PRAYERS FROM FRANCISCAN HEARTS

PRAYERS
FROM
FRANCISCAN
HEARTS

CONTEMPORARY

REFLECTIONS

FROM

WOMEN

AND

MEN

PAULA PEARCE, S.F.O.

ST. ANTHONY MESSENGER PRESS
Cincinnati, Ohio

Scripture passages have been taken from *New Revised Standard Version Bible,* copyright ©1989 by the Division of Christian Education of the National Council of the Churches of Christ in the U.S.A., and used by permission. All rights reserved.

Excerpts from *Francis of Assisi: Early Documents, Volumes I* and *II,* Regis J. Armstrong, O.F.M. CAP., J.A. Wayne Hellmann, O.F.M. CONV., William J. Short, O.F.M., eds., ©1999, reprinted with permission of New City Press.

Cover and book design by Mark Sullivan.

LIBRARY OF CONGRESS CATALOGING-IN-PUBLICATION DATA
Prayers from Franciscan hearts : contemporary reflections from women and men / edited by Paula Pearce.
p. cm.
ISBN 978-0-86716-741-2 (pbk. : alk. paper) 1. Franciscans—Prayers and devotions. 2. Franciscans—Prayers and devotions. I. Pearce, Paula.

BX2188.F7P73 2007
242—dc22

2007024580

ISBN 978-0-86716-741-2

Published by St. Anthony Messenger Press
28 W. Liberty St.
Cincinnati, OH 45202
www.AmericanCatholic.org

Printed in the United States of America.

Printed on acid-free paper.

07 08 09 10 11 5 4 3 2 1

CONTENTS

AT THE TIME THAT SAINTS FRANCIS AND CLARE LIVED, PILGRIMAGE LITERATURE was a large body of writing, especially accounts of pilgrimages to Jerusalem, which was *the* medieval pilgrimage. The Jerusalem pilgrimage was understood as going to the actual geographical place, but it was also seen as the journey of the soul to God. It was the pilgrim soul on the way to heaven.

Those who wrote of these pilgrimages wrote differing kinds of accounts. Some were logs, some were guidebooks and others simply the story of their own pilgrimage.

In this book the structure for the writers' focus is the pilgrimage to Assisi in the footsteps of Francis and Clare. The writing comprises mainly prayers that the writers were moved to record, and at times there are brief narratives of what happened in a given place. But whatever genre the writers here employ, what emerges is an account from their Franciscan hearts.

The reader feels he or she is eavesdropping on an intimate colloquy between the pilgrim and God, or the pilgrim and Francis or Clare. In listening in, the reader's own pilgrimage memories are jarred, whether or not he or she has been to Assisi. I suspect that one who has not been to Assisi will, by the end of the book, find a reason to embark on that principal Franciscan pilgrimage.

Some of the writings here aspire to art, some are simply the spontaneous outpourings of the heart confronted with the lives and places of Francis and Clare of Assisi. Some are prayers, others meditations, but all attest to the power of the Franciscan charism to change lives, to inspire and to elicit words of gratitude and joy that the pilgrim soul feels impelled to preserve in the written word.

Medieval pilgrimage literature continues here in the words of modern pilgrims journeying back to the same Middle Ages that saw the inception of pilgrim accounts. In the Middle Ages these principal places were Jerusalem, Rome and the shrine of St. Michael at Monte Gargano south of Rome. They were called the *Deus* (God) Pilgrimage, which was Jerusalem; the *Homo* (Human) Pilgrimage, which was Rome; and the *Angelus* (Angel) Pilgrimage to the shrine of St. Michael. Ortolana, the mother of Saint Clare of Assisi, made all three pilgrimages, and now in these pages are the records of pilgrimages back to the place she started from: Assisi, the center toward which all Franciscan pilgrimages converge, the lodestone of the Franciscan pilgrim soul.

Murray Bodo, O.F.M.

THIS BOOK WAS CONCEIVED TO FORM PART OF THE CELEBRATIONS FOR THE eighth centenary of the approval given by Pope Innocent III to the simple form of life proposed by Saint Francis of Assisi and his first companions. It has grown into this compilation of original prayers and reflections, composed by contemporary Franciscans and others who have been touched by the Franciscan charism from several different countries.

With the idea in mind of a pilgrimage as "conversion," I have arranged the chapters as "stations," or movements toward conversion as it pertains to the lives of Francis and Clare. Christ asked those who listened to him to repent, meaning to seek a radical change in the direction of their lives by turning their hearts away from evil and back to God. Sincere repentance is accompanied by a genuine desire and firm resolution to change one's way of life. In order to begin the process of radical daily conversion, Christians need faith and hope in God's mercy and grace.

Saints Francis and Clare of Assisi received the inspiration and grace to surrender their lives totally to God and became devoted and faithful followers of Christ. The stations of this pilgrimage visit places that marked significant stages on their journeys back to God. Each station opens with an introduction, giving information about the place and its context within their distinctive journeys. Contributions, relevant to the theme of the station, follow. The station closes with simple suggestions for further reflection as well as pertinent scriptural references.

All Christians start their faith journey at baptism. Let us begin this pilgrim journey at the baptismal font of the Cathedral of San Rufino in Assisi, where Clare and Francis were baptized.

THE RICH AND POWERFUL OF ASSISI CHOSE THE HIGHEST GROUND WITHIN THE city walls on which to build their mansions and their church. San Rufino now, as then, presents a commanding façade. The interior of the church, with its ornate sepulchers, dedicated plaques and military insignias, further reflects the aspirations of its parishioners and all around the piazza are the elegant houses of the aristocratic elite.

The history behind Rufino's prominence is largely a legend that dates back centuries. The legend tells us that in the eighth century, the sarcophagus holding the remains of the first Bishop of Assisi, Rufino, who was tortured and drowned by the Romans, was found in the river where he was martyred. The relics were then moved to a small church, built where the piazza of San Rufino now stands. As Assisi grew in power, its citizens were eager to find out more about their patron saint. In the eleventh century his sarcophagus was brought into the city. Bishop Ugo planned to install it in the cathedral church of Santa Maria Maggiore, lower down the hill, adjacent

3

to his palace. However, a strange force prevented the bearers of the sarcophagus from reaching the cathedral. They were instead guided to the church of San Rufino. Soon after San Rufino became the center of ecclesiastical power and eventually replaced Santa Maria Maggiore as the cathedral church of Assisi. There was rivalry, and even hostility, between the leaders and followers of the two churches—just one of the tumultuous social and political upheavals of the time.

Another struggle was between the established aristocracy and the rising class of wealthy traders, and Clare's and Francis' families were no exception. Clare was from an aristocratic family. Francis' father, Pietro Bernardone, was a wealthy trader of cloth. Both families were in bitter battles to maintain their social standing.

Yet, despite their different social classes and the resulting power struggle, both Francis' and Clare's families were Catholic. Their social lives were interwoven into the liturgical year and the great Christian feasts. Like many children of privileged classes who were taught to read, Clare and Francis read the psalms. Additionally, their early learning was rooted in the social mores and political allegiances of their families.

As a child Francis excelled in social graces. He was confident, sociable and successful in trade, which pleased his father greatly. He commanded the love and respect of his peers. They were drawn to his enthusiasm and commitment. The young, valiant Francis aspired to be the most courageous of knights, ready to fight and to give his life for a cause he perceived as being noble and right. Eventually, he entered into battle against the Perugians, and was imprisoned after the battle of Collestrada. His confinement was traumatic, and as traumas so often are, it was a turning point for young Francis.

During his imprisonment, Francis began to question the meaning of his life and its direction. He began to question his role in his faith, to ponder the essential teachings of Christ and the ethos of materialism and worldly success. After his release and upon his return to Assisi, Francis sought solitude and felt a great need to pray. He begged for God's guidance, not in the proud nave of San Rufino, but in its quiet crypt. Eventually, he looked to a desolate cave outside the city walls as refuge for his questioning soul. Spiritually and physically, he had moved, taking the first steps of his pilgrim journey.

CONTRIBUTIONS

THE BAPTISMAL FONT IN THE CHURCH AT SAN RUFINO

In 1976 I took my first Franciscan Pilgrimage to Assisi. I stayed for a week at San Damiano Friary, which was the novitiate for the Province of Assisi. There were many wonderful moments as I visited the holy places so important in the lives of Francis and Clare and for the whole of Franciscan history.

Several times I visited the Church of San Rufino, the parish church of Francis and Clare. Here was the very place Francis had preached the lenten sermons that so affected Clare. Here was the spot where Clare received the palm branches from the bishop's hand on that Palm Sunday, in March 1212. Just hours later, she left her home with a servant in the dark of night to make her way to the Portiuncula. I was standing in the very spot where all this happened.

But what touched me most of all was being right next to the baptismal font where Francis and Clare received the sacrament of baptism as infants. I was able to reach out and touch that holy font. As infants, of course they could not have known what was going on in their lives and their hearts at that sacramental moment. Francis could have no idea what the Lord would call him to twenty-four years later in 1206 when the Lord spoke to him from the San Damiano chapel cross and urged him to rebuild that broken-down church. Could Clare know that eighteen years after her baptism she would leave her family to join the family of Francis? Their baptism put them on the path of a very special journey that would change the lives of countless men and women for the next eight centuries and beyond.

But then it dawned on me that the only reason I myself was standing there as a Franciscan was because Francis and Clare were held as infants for baptism at that very same place. I might well be a religious and a priest, but except for Francis and Clare, I and all of us Franciscans would not be who we are, doing what we are doing, and calling Francis and Clare our father and mother if it were not for that sacred moment at the font in San Rufino, which mysteriously still touches our own lives 800 years later. It is truly amazing what one single moment in time can mean not just for future centuries but for all eternity.

James Van Vurst, O.F.M.

. . .

Call to Assisi 2003

If you have never walked amongst those pleasant Umbrian hills,
Walked them in blazing sunshine, or during wintry chills,
Walked in the steps of Francis, of Clare and many more,
Who chose to be Franciscan, to love and adore the Lord,
Our Almighty God, our guardian and our friend, who
Of his loving kindness, with us his time does spend.
Then, this I advocate my friend,
Walk now, don't hesitate,

Let Clare and Francis talk with you,
Let them both share your weight
They'll hold your hand,
They'll listen
Help you to cogitate.

But if you are a happy soul,
Who's walked this walk before,
Thank him, who made the flowers,
For calling you once more
To walk again in Umbria,
To feel that stirring breeze
That sometimes,
When it's strongest,
Returns you to your knees.
Sit and chat with Francis,
Tell Clare the things you need,
Ask them to show you patiently
How to nourish your spiritual seed.
How to grow and flourish
To blossom like a flower
So others see your smiling face,
Bathed by sweet graces' showers.

Come all, the confirmed and the new
In Assisi your spiritual self renew.

Kim Pemberton

ASSISI

This place lets the heart spin
Run free, unpin,
Till all within
Is filled with light.

Light, sound of bell,
Both weave their spell,
Church, oratory and cell
Proclaim the Lord above.

I too must do my part.
This is the place to start,
Open with joy my heart
To Holy Spirit, dove.

John Gordon Clark

. . .

I FEEL SO AT HOME HERE

I feel so at home here,
No room for any fear.
God's love is everywhere,
Basilicas, nature, the very air...
The lovely pastry shops and gelato
Singing in the streets and visiting pilgrims impromptu.
All are open to God's story
Beauty pointing to His Glory...
What a holy time this is for sure,
Experiencing God's love so pure.

Sometimes it is hard to sleep
With my soul at the summit peak.
So I pray into the night—
For all I love and hold tight.
God is blessing them for me,
As a gift, precious and free.

Sister Delores Wisnicky

. . .

AUTUMN IN ASSISI

Autumn is just beginning.

The golden light is shafting through the trees on Mount Subasio
And greens are interspersed with reds and yellows.

In the valley gray-green olive groves, their shadows mingling, move
gently in the breeze
And cypress trees stand sentinel around the cloisters.

The walled city itself radiates light—a medieval city, the very stones
singing out
The message of humility and love to all around.

The Churches throw their lengthening shadows across the piazzas
Where pilgrims sit, sipping a café latte in the dwindling afternoon.

Franciscan Brothers walk the streets. "Pace e Bene" the greeting of
800 years,
Smiles of welcome shining from their faces.

Signs of earthquake damage and rebuilding
But people go about their daily business
And the spirit of the Saint lives on
Walking alongside every Pilgrim, as they wend their way

Up steep steps climbing ever upward or down through narrow streets
now deep in shadow.

The sun sets earlier now behind the mountains across the valley
The great Basilica glows in all its glory
Holding at its heart the body of this little Saint
Whose whole life radiated with humility and love,
Poverty and obedience to God.

The autumnal sunset fades, but a translucent light keeps watch
As though Saint Francis' blessing on this fair city
Is reiterated every evening for eternity.

Imogen Vignoles

. . .

ASSISI: A PLACE OF PEACEFUL DANCE

Not many who visit the small Italian town of Assisi are able to escape
its enchantment. For some it is the medieval walls whose stones
speak of another time and place. Still others find the panoramic vis-
tas of the Spoleto valley to be breathtaking. For pilgrims of many
faiths, it is a holy place that radiates a spiritual energy of universal
appeal crossing religious, ethnic, economic and political barriers. For
my family and fellow Franciscans who journeyed with me, it was an
opportunity to find our spiritual home.

We happened to be there on the fourth anniversary of September
11. My wife, daughter, father-in-law and I trekked up countless brick
and stone steps to the upper walls surrounding Assisi. Helicopters
loaded with TV reporters and cameras whirled above us, disturbing
what could have been a contemplative walk. Up ahead perched on
the top of the hill stood the Rocca Maggiore, a large, German-style,
feudal castle where the emperor Frederick II of Swabia spent several

years of his childhood. The castle casts a seductive shadow over the entire city, sharing the skyline with the beautiful Basilica of St. Francis, reminding pilgrims of Assisi's long war-torn and violent past. Crowds gathered outside the fortress walls surrounded by sculptures, paintings and music, speaking about peace. Collages documenting recent war atrocities were interspersed with icons of a modern Madonna, Gandhi and various saints and martyrs, named and unnamed.

On our way down, we were greeted by hundreds of joyful peace marchers of every color and ideology who had begun their walk thirty miles away in the town of Perugia, historically the enemy of Assisi. Europeans of different nationalities playfully waved banners displaying the medieval coats of arms of their ancestral homes— poking fun at the military connotations. Throngs of young children, teens, parents and grandparents squeezed through narrow streets. African dancers, hikers with communist flags, Americans and religious of many kinds paraded together with joyful smiles.

Later that night, our tired group collected our thoughts and prayers for the day after our Eucharist together. Our twelve-year-old daughter, Rachel, the youngest sage in our group, commented about the peace march and how good she felt meeting happy people, especially children her own age, who thought like her. She said she was tired of the boys at school who talk endlessly about their video war games and aren't interested in her point of view. Our group gave thanks for Rachel's newfound strength and voice. We also recalled how Francis helped bring down the feudal system in Europe by requiring his early followers to not bear arms. That night, we all left for our separate rooms at St. Anthony's Guesthouse with a little more hope and peace in our hearts. We had, however momentarily, given peace a dance!

Stephen Best

THE FRANCISCAN CALLING

Patched robe of Saint Francis
Seen in Assisi
Says it all—
Hear the call.
Go out into highways
And byways of life
Draw Christ near
To those who will hear
Transform yourself,
By God's grace,
To His will,

Hear the call.
Saint Clare in convent
Lies there still
Tended by prayerful Sisters,
Bound sweetly in Holy Eucharist.

Earthquake at Assisi,
God's warning perhaps
To mend His Church,
Reassert the Faith.
Brothers and Sisters of Christ,
One in Christ's Blood
To change the world
Before Heaven comes
Drawing it near.

Hazel Smith

FOR REFLECTION

1. Renew your baptismal promises or any personal commitment you have made during your faith journey.

2. Reflect on a memory, a person or a place that has special significance for you.

SUGGESTED SCRIPTURE

Matthew 3:11–17; 28:16–20

Station Two: The Seeker

Mount Subasio rises above Assisi. Pathways lead up the tree-covered mountainside that conceals clefts, hollows and caves, ideal for shelter or solitude. This station marks the beginning of a period of prayer when Francis sought solitary places to come face to face with his inner self and to seek discernment. "The First Life" by Thomas of Celano, describes the listlessness that dogged Francis' convalescence.

> When he had recovered a little and, with the support of a cane, had begun to walk about here and there...he went outside one day and began to gaze upon the surrounding countryside with greater interest. But the beauty of the fields, the delight of the vineyards, and whatever else was beautiful to see could offer him no delight at all.... From that day he began to regard himself as worthless and to hold in some contempt what he had previously held as admirable and lovable, though not completely or genuinely. For he had not yet been freed from the *bonds of vanities* nor *had he thrown off from his neck the yoke* of degrading servitude.[1]

During this solitary period, Francis had one companion with whom he could discuss matters of the soul. He underwent a radical inner transformation of soul. From an initial feeling of loss and wretchedness, Francis was moved to seek repentance for his sins. Although he was gradually able to accept God's mercy, he remained in fear that he would continue to live in sinfulness.

The man of God...was accustomed to enter the cave...and inspired by a new and extraordinary spirit he would pray to his *Father in secret....* He prayed with all his heart that the eternal and true God guide his way and *teach him to do His will.* He endured great suffering in his soul, and he was not able to rest until he accomplished in action what he had conceived in his heart. Different thoughts followed one after another, and their relentlessness severely disturbed him.... He repented that he had sinned so grievously and that he had offended *the eyes of majesty....* [H]e was not yet fully confident of refraining from future [transgressions].[2]

Francis grappled with himself until he fully experienced the power of God's mercy. He was suddenly overwhelmed when he became conscious of the greatness of God's love. This filled him with indescribable joy. He had found the hidden treasure promised in the gospels. A new strength enabled him to return to life in Assisi where he believed that he could do great and noble things.

God did not move Francis too quickly. Nor did Francis make a complete break once and for all from the earthly things he enjoyed. The "Legend of the Three Companions" describes what happened when Francis tried to resume his former lifestyle, treating his friends to a banquet and leading them in their after-dinner revels. He was suddenly struck by a sense of all-consuming tenderness which overwhelmed him completely and made him stop in his tracks. His friends assumed that he was thinking about a woman, which Francis found himself saying was true. Much later he realized that this bride represented both the religion and the lifestyle of poverty that he was finally to adopt.

CONTRIBUTIONS

REDEMPTION

Disoriented
As if separated from
the Way
grasping for some
stabilizing branch

Yearning to see
I had lost sight
desperate to know love
forgetting how

upside down
striving for uprightness
afraid of the inside
shutting all doors.

Then subtle
light
like gentle fingers
that unfold
the eastern sky
pointed the path home.

Lynda Maraby

Breath of God

O breath of God, come set me free
From weighing burdens set on me.
Unforgiveness keeps us apart
When anger resides within my heart.

Make me willing to see my plight;
Open my eyes and give me sight...
That I may look within my soul
To see what keeps me from the goal
Of love of neighbor and of self.

Let me not too busy be...
To sit,
To ponder,
To stay with Thee....
Until my heart does soften more
And I can open a once closed door.

Jean Mahan

.   .   .

The Word—a God who can only love

The Lord calls in silence.
In a world of peace, God's word comes
like the descent of a quiet, velvet night.

There is no special way to speak to God,
no particular way that says everything.
What a marvelous experience,

to be in the presence of God—
and what is adequate is silence.

God reads the heart
and proclaims marvels to people who love God,
even to those who may not know God.

God writes, etches our names
on the palm of God's hand
where they are seen when God raises
those hands before his eyes.
If the world were to stop tomorrow,
God would still be present to me.
Should I die or no longer be able
to speak, or see, or walk,
God would still exist and love me.

If all the things I have done,
all the people I have met,
all the panels I have nailed to walls,
the cabinets I have created,
the words I have written,
the sermons I have given,
if they would all disappear,
God would still be present
and God would still love me,
for our God is a faithful God.

It is difficult for a person
who is full of "self"
to acknowledge such a loving God.
It would mean acknowledging

that there is Someone whom I cannot control,
Someone whom I cannot teach,
Someone whom I cannot stop
from loving me
and calling me to new life.

Despite whatever I may do,
God continues to be God,
continues to love me,
continues to call me to love
so that God's will may be done
on earth as it is in heaven.

A proud person is blind.
It is a blindness that comes from the
brilliant shine of his/her own sun.
It is too bright
and blinds our eyes to the Light of the world.
How strange it is, to realize
that two different lights
have two different effects.
One leads to blindness,
the other to light and vision.
Lord, heal the blindness caused by my own sun.
Open me to the light of your Son.

Make me a Eucharist,
someone who is always thanking you
for the wonder of you
Light and the Word-made-flesh. Amen.

Lester Bach

Dear Lord, help me to cope with the reality of myself

Dear Lord, help me to cope with the reality of myself,
Help me to be aware of the things within myself
which push me away from you;
Let me take to myself as truth
the fact of your all-consuming love
And give me the hope
that comes from knowing that my sins are forgiven. Amen.

John McLeod

. . .

A House Divided

I have discovered a part of myself that I am deeply ashamed of, and yet it is so much a part of me that the exorcising will be immensely painful. I am divided against myself.

This is not simply a bad habit or sin that I can "stop doing." It's woven into the fabric of my personality. Only You, Jesus, can cast out this demon. Yet this demon holds me back from approaching you in true Franciscan humility.

O Lord, help me to want to be rid of it. Last night I dreamed of a terribly forceful wind that was driving everyone into the sea. There was only one person who was being driven in the opposite direction, and this person was trying to save the others by holding them against the fierce wind. It was a losing battle.

This was I, Lord, trying to save the parts of myself that are possessed by the demon. I couldn't do it. Lord, I beg of you to still the winds of self-destruction that push against my coming closer to you. Please Lord, cast out my demons. I am exhausted, and can go no further without you.

Miriam Kennedy

CHILD OF A KING

Father, just how long
Can I sustain this lie,
Denial of the truth of who I am?
It is as if, like Francis,
I'd been cursed,
And chosen for myself
A beggar to father me,
Refusing to acknowledge
I'm the child of a King.

But all the lies I've lived,
The deceit,
The guarded silence of my soul,
Are being shattered,
As the chains fall off my limbs
The gag removed,
And I am clothed in the naked freedom
Of a child of God.

My real self, now recognized,
Demands a freedom to obey,
Not slavishly,
But with delirious joy.
Bubbling up
To soar into the sunlight,
Where the hidden one
Now calls me to the shelter of his side.

He calls for rings and gowns
To celebrate a feast for me.

I find it hard to understand myself.
Just why did I believe the lies
That kept me groveling in pigsties.
No more like a ragged gypsy will I roam.
I am the child of a King.
I'm home.

Maureen Maguire

. . .

AS SAINT FRANCIS DID

As Saint Francis did, may we keep our eyes and thoughts and hearts and praises lifted to the glorious mysteries on high; rather than downcast to our toils here plodding upon this dirt floor of creation. Lord, Grant us through grace the strength and courage we need this day, that together with the hope of our faith we may confront our challenges, and in so doing learn and grow all that we can from them regardless of their outcome. Draw us toward your sacred wisdom and its revelation that yours is not only the light of the world and the light of life, but also the light of our salvation. Empower us to live as examples of your Word in this world of darkness that others may be drawn toward your light. Wherein, all who are enveloped by nature's magnificence, and awakened by our senses blessed bestowance, can but stand speechless before creation both beholder and beholden.

As I kneel before you now I do so humbly, bearing the yoke of my sins. Lord, in your mercy help me rise to become the man I can be— the man you created me to be. With your Holy Spirit as my staff, though I will falter in my travels and travails, I shall never fall.

God of all that was and is and will be, you are my comfort and my joy realized in conquering my weakness thru your divinity. Lead me forward to create of this life the foundation your perfect heart desires.

Gracious Saint Francis, I ask that you render before heaven's throne my petition on behalf of a world writhing. That all heartache be replaced with healing, that all animosity be displaced by generosity, and that love's embrace soothes anger's torment.

In the name of the Father, the Son and the Holy Spirit I pray. Amen.

A.M. Salvatore

For Reflection

1. Set aside enough time to listen to God as you reflect on your life.
2. Create a sacred space in your home or close by that you can go to spend time alone with God.

Suggested Scripture

Hosea 2:14

Mark 6:31–32

Luke 4:1

Notes

[1] "The Life of Saint Francis" in *Francis of Assisi, Early Documents*, volume I, *The Saint*, Regis J. Armstrong, J. A. Wayne Hellmann, and William J. Short, eds. (New York: New City Press, 1999), p. 185. Hereafter this volume will be referred to as *FA:ED I* followed by page numbers.

[2] *FA:ED I*, "The Life of Saint Francis," p. 187.

STATION THREE: THE EMBRACE OF THE LEPER

AT THIS STATION, FRANCIS CONQUERED A PERSONAL FEAR, A HORROR THAT repelled him. He struggled with an inner enemy that was blocking him from true freedom and was a barrier between him and God. In the "Major Life," Bonaventure places this encounter with the leper early in Francis' conversion. Francis had not broken away from his roots. In fact he was still riding on horseback, a symbol of social status and wealth:

> One day, therefore, while he was riding his horse through the plain that lies below the city of Assisi, he met a leper. This unforeseen encounter struck him with not a little horror. Recalling the plan of perfection he had already conceived in his mind, and remembering that he must first conquer himself if he wanted to become a *knight of Christ*, he dismounted from his horse and ran to kiss him. As the leper stretched out his hand as if to receive something, he gave him money with a kiss. Immediately mounting his horse, however, and turning all around, even though the open plain stretched clear in all direction, he could not see the leper anywhere. He began, therefore, *filled with wonder and joy*, to sing praises to the Lord, while proposing, because of this, to embark always on the greater.[1]

Francis' embrace of the leper is a powerful icon in the Franciscan tradition. People tend to think of it as the singular episode in Francis' conversion. In his "Testament," in which he looked back over the most significant episodes in his life, Francis singled out the service of lepers:

> The Lord granted me, Brother Francis, to begin to do penance in this way: While I was in sin, it seemed very bitter to me to see lepers. And the Lord Himself led me among them and I had mercy on them. And when I left them that which seemed bitter to me was changed into sweetness of soul.[2]

A special liturgical rite was composed for use when lepers were cast out of society because they were regarded as dead to the community. They lived on the plain, outside the city walls. By association with lepers, Francis made himself as one of them in the eyes of the townspeople. To embrace a leper symbolized rejection of all that Francis could have embraced in Assisi—power, wealth, prestige and success.

During his solitude, Francis had acknowledged his great sinfulness, shed tears of repentance and found God's mercy. He could embrace his sinfulness in all its horror. He now believed that he had been truly and totally forgiven. He saw his true self, his identity, as a leper, a great sinner, who was loved by God unconditionally, and who could do nothing himself to earn such immense, all-consuming love.

Through God's compassionate mercy, Francis experienced inner freedom. This is how the Lord taught him to go out and do the same. Once he honestly accepted God's love, he could embrace other "lepers" with mercy. He now saw everything from a new perspective and responded, with thanks and praise, in humble gratitude.

He understood that the Lord had the same unconditional love for everyone. God looked at him, leper that he was, and loved him. He began to serve lepers in and around Assisi. He was able to see Christ in everyone, especially in the suffering.

CONTRIBUTIONS

FRANCIS AND THE LEPER

When he embraces the leper, Francis does something very simple and yet so powerful that it changes his life forever. He does something that people very rarely do, something that he, Francis, had never done before. Why did Francis need to embrace a leper, when like the rest of us he had sought for life and God in light, not in darkness, in sweetness, not in pain, in joy, not in sorrow?

It is the voice of Jesus that confuses him, compels him to go where he does not want to go:

> Francis, everything you loved carnally and desired to have, you must despise and hate, if you wish to know my will. Because once you begin doing this, what before seemed delightful and sweet will be unbearable and bitter; and what before made you shudder will offer you great sweetness and enormous delight.[3]

And so, when Francis next meets a leper he forces himself to dismount. In this way he approaches an unknown world, both within himself and without. This is not to say that Francis had never responded generously to a human being before; he had done so many times. He had been generous when it was easy, with his friends at parties, plying them with good food, company and wine. He was familiar with that kind of giving. And more recently, he had started to train himself to be kind to beggars; he had shared his food with them, even his clothing. One day in Rome he exchanged his clothes with a poor man and stood at the doors of the church of St. Peter, begging for alms.

And yet to approach a leper was more than this. Francis was popular, attractive, his body free from sores. A leper belonged to the living dead. A leper was hideous, contagious. He had no recognized existence. He was greeted on all sides by rejection and fear. To touch a leper was to risk entering the leper's world. It was to risk becoming like the leper. This was the kind of giving Francis was not good at, the kind he did not want to do.

Francis had always refused to look at lepers. He had held his nose and turned away. In this way he protected himself and the world he knew, a world of songs and laughter, a world in which heroism won the prize of life, of love, of happiness. No one would applaud if Francis kissed a leper. To look at the leper meant to see him, to see him as a suffering human being. To see the leper meant that Francis must include him in his own vision of the world. There had never been a leper in Francis' world before. To look at the leper meant to look at Francis, to see in Francis something Francis did not want to see.

Francis looks at the leper and has compassion. In seeing the leper he sees himself, a disfigured, much-loved child of God. He embraces the leper and leaves his world.

Sister Ruth Agnes

. . .

KISS A LEPER?

Kiss a leper? On the lips? Are you kidding? I wonder if this was Saint Francis of Assisi's initial reaction when faced with what it took to live out his desire to "get into the skin" of Jesus. Francis was sickened at the sight of lepers and must have felt horrified when this one appeared in his path. Even so, it was with little hesitation that he got down from his horse, put his arms around the leper and kissed him on the lips. In that kiss Francis' heart was transformed, enabling him to begin to live among and lovingly serve his society's outcasts. Many years ago when the AIDS epidemic first began, I was one who had little compassion for those with the dreaded disease and I certainly could not see myself ministering to AIDS patients. Not much was known about AIDS at that time, and there was great fear that mere contact with an AIDS-infected person would spread the disease. It was hard for me to understand why a nun in our parish would leave her parish ministries in order to work among AIDS patients. It was even harder to understand when I learned how much she loved her new ministry to these "lepers" of our society. Years later, in response to a spiritual yearning, I was led to the Secular Franciscan Order. Since then the ways of Saint Francis of Assisi have changed my heart to one of greater acceptance and love. Today one of my personal apostolates is ministering to the dear residents in our community's home for people with HIV/AIDS. Together we go to the store, the bank or wherever they want to go. Together we share meals, stories and hugs. Together we feel the love of our Lord in one another. Recently I was asked to clean a bathroom where an AIDS patient had just died. At first sight, my stomach got queasy, but it took only a moment to get off my high horse and onto my hands and knees to begin cleaning. Reflecting on the experience on my way home, I knew I had just kissed the leper on the lips. I also knew that I would go back and do it again.

Gail Campbell

Do Not Be Afraid

Francis, man of courage!
You met your fears head on...
the leper, brother wolf,
   sister death.
What message do you have for me,
so often afraid?
Look your fear in the eyes,
take a risk!
Don't let your fear conquer you,
   conquer it!
Even the countless daily little fears
noone knows about.
And the worst fear of all,
   tomorrow.
Lord, let me live today,
just this one day, fearlessly!

Monica Sheeran

. . .

Saint Francis and the Good Samaritan

One of Saint Francis' thirteenth-century biographers, Thomas of
Celano, tells us that as a result of Francis' rejection of a beggar who
came to his father's shop, Francis resolved not to deny *anyone*. It is
typical of Francis that in order to redeem himself he goes to the
extreme and takes literally "anyone" and thus from then on not only
helps beggars, but dismounts from his horse (an act of humility) and
kisses a leper (an outcast from society), and then, according to
another biographer, Francis takes a large sum of money and goes to a

leper hospital and kisses the hand of each leper and gives them alms. In the Gospel parable of the Good Samaritan in Luke, the beaten man for whom the Samaritan stops is reaching out for help (10:30–37). The leper, likewise, stretched out his hands for alms and received both money and a kiss from Francis. The Good Samaritan cared for the beaten man, took him to an inn and paid the innkeeper for the man's board and lodging. In Francis' case it is as if he has to go farther, to lepers, in order for him to complete his penance for his rejection of the beggar. He does not just care for the leper as the Good Samaritan does for the wounded man; Francis goes to the furthest extreme and lives with them.

The sources for the story of Francis embracing the leper help us to understand the humility of Francis who dismounted to kiss the leper; both of which are acts of humility. Francis becomes an *alter Christus* (Christ-like) who kisses, cares for and allies himself with lepers (a leper being a medieval metaphor for the rejected, humiliated, crucified Christ). This act of Francis is an outward sign of his penance and the fact that he cares for the afflicted ("I showed mercy on them," he tells us in his *Testament*). He thus becomes at one (atoned) with the leper, that is the crucified Christ.

Simon Spikin

. . .

THE SHADOW OF GOD'S LIGHT IN THE LIFE OF BROTHER PIO

The evening sun cast long shadows and Brother Pio saw his own among those that were formed by the branches of the trees that surrounded the wooded glade. As he moved, his shadow moved. It copied every action that he made. Brother Pio thought to himself, "Through Brother Sun, God has provided me with a companion."

Before he had noticed his shadow, Brother Pio had been meditating on the life of humankind on earth. He wondered, "Why is it that so many people lived for the hour and the gratification of self in material things"? He knew how much disappointment was suffered by them, particularly where God had been excluded from their lives. He then started to wonder if the founder of his order, Saint Francis of Assisi, might have had a similar encounter to the one he had just experienced. Could it have been that the young Francis Bernardone, when he looked into his own shadow, had first seen and met Lady Poverty?

It struck Brother Pio that whatever happened to Saint Francis, the human shadow was the perfect symbol of Lady Poverty. The beauty is in its emptiness and its captivating mystery. It exists without a material being of its own. It moves in perfect harmony. It is completely attached to a person and does not leave even when it cannot be seen. It is a reminder of the Almighty, because it is through the direct light of Brother Sun, the image in nature of the one true God, that it exists. Brother Pio remembered how Saint Francis had welcomed Lady Poverty into his life and how he had delighted in her presence and embraced her. He understood now how his own shadow would help him follow in Saint Francis' footsteps.

As he stood there, Brother Pio's mind started to think again about his brothers and sisters. They had this same gift of a shadow as he had. Their shadows, too, could also serve them as a reminder of God's presence in their lives, a God to whom they should give thanks for their existence.

Everything is God's and God's gift to us while we are upon this earth. This includes seeking and doing His will. Yes, the personal shadow, its emptiness of material wealth is a constant reminder of the richness of the spiritual wealth God wishes to bestow on us; if only we empty ourselves of our own self-centeredness.

As he walked back toward the friary, Brother Pio made a resolution that he would tell everyone he met about this experience and encourage people to embrace their own shadows. Like Saint Francis, Brother Pio wanted all people to enjoy the inner peace and happiness God wishes to give them and which they all crave, but do not know how to obtain.

Allan Simpson

. . .

THE SUNLIGHT WAS DANCING

The sunlight was dancing upon the street as the stooped old woman made her way through the streets of Rome to the streetlamp at a busy intersection near the church of St. John Lateran. Here she sat with her earthly possessions. She would spend the morning calling out to those around her in a quiet, gentle voice, "In the name of God, I beg you, have mercy on me." So busy in their own thoughts, some didn't even see her. Some glanced her way but kept on going. Yet, she persistently cried out for the bustling crowd to have mercy on her, for she needed to buy something to eat.

Suddenly a poor man, small in stature, approached her. He reached into the folds of his clothing and produced a small loaf of bread. He stooped down and gazed onto the face of the old woman. Into her hands, he reverently placed the bread. His rough hands embraced hers as she received the bread from him. Silence filled the air and time stood still as the poor man and the beggar woman embraced one another. Her eyes danced with gratitude and on her joy-filled face was an expression of knowing she was loved by this man. The poor man continued to enfold her in his gaze and his eyes looked upon the beggar woman with love. Francis had found his loving God in the beggar woman of Rome.

Sister Mary Keman

INVITATORY

Stretch out your soul
On the bed of my wounds
And rest there
In open abandonment.
Vulnerable to the pain
Of all earth's children
Resist the instinctual
Drawing inwards
Of self preservation
Accept the blurring of boundaries
Truly they are not
Except in the minds of humankind
Erectors of barricades
Attempting to keep away
Whomever they think will
Steal the security
They cling to.
Awakened to the lie
Don't fall back asleep
As before.
Rest in me
Fully awake.

Debra Freeman

Lord Christ, Let Me Feel Your Touch

Lord Christ, let me feel your touch.

Touch my voice, teach me to say, "Abba, Father."

Teach me to say, "I love you." Lord Christ, let me feel your touch. Touch me when I am afraid, anxious, discouraged, apathetic.

Cast out my fears, calm me, give me hope and purpose. Lord Christ, let me feel your touch. As you were present to the disciples on the road to Emmaus.

Be present to me in the breaking of the bread. As you forgave the thief on the cross and the woman caught in adultery. You have forgiven me. Touch me again so I can forgive others. As you healed those you touched in Galilee you have healed me.

Make me a channel for your healing love to flow through to others. You have called me, included me, invited me to your party.

Help me never to exclude anyone. You know what it is to weep. Touch me when I need to cry, So the healing tears may flow. You have allowed me to touch the hem of your garment.

Now touch my whole being so I may be transformed. Lord Christ, let me feel your touch. Let others feel your touch through me. Lord Christ, let me feel your touch.

Sue Tidwell

. . .

Franciscan Moment

Saint Francis! You've been a role model for me for as long as I can remember. My father's middle name was Francis, my brother's name was Francis. We were taught at a young age to venerate and imitate your saintly ways.

The opportunity for me to become a secular Franciscan did not occur until I was well past middle age, and I flew at that chance. The honor of becoming a part of you was one of my greatest experiences. I was truly blessed. The excitement, the anticipation on that day was so great I compared it to my wedding day forty some years before. This day would also change my life forever. If only I could have seen ahead just a few minutes....

When the hugs, handshakes and happy tears were done, my friend, who had also become a secular Franciscan on that day, and I floated down the steps of the church on our newfound sanctity. At the bottom of the steps a man suddenly stood before us. He was obviously down on his luck. He took off his cap and held out his hand and asked if we could please help him. Could we give him a little money? And what did we two new secular Franciscans do? We told him the nuns' convent was just around the corner and that they would be happy to help him. We left him standing there, hand outstretched.

The full impact of what we had just done hit us as we were driving home. The guilt stabbed deep. A better way of putting it was: What had we just *not* done?

After a while the embarrassment, the painful guilt, subsided into a dull ache and the humor of the situation, if you could call it that, surfaced. Being two women who had lived full lives, raised our families, welcomed grandchildren, celebrated joys and suffered heartbreak and were now looking old age in the eye, we did what we always do. We laughed! What else was there to do?

For several years we practiced our Franciscanhood. We prayed, we loved, we gave where we could but too many times for coincidence something would remind us of the humiliation, the pain, of that awful moment by the church steps. We'd bury our real feelings deep inside and we'd laugh again.

Then one day we two secular Franciscans were visiting with our new parish priest about the incident. Our laughter was suddenly cut short by his soft powerful words. "Maybe that man was Saint Francis!"

Saint Francis, was it you?

Madeleine Gilmore

. . .

WITHIN A TOMB

Within a tomb
I am conceived.
My hands, my feet,
They are completing.
My body growing
Not yet born
But yet...! I have a being
I am alive; I live
I am not allowed
To have my life
My heart beats
My body grows
Yet!
Here I live and die
I am termed *abortion*.

K. McGrath

WHERE ARE THE CHILDREN?

Where are the children?
Where did they go?
O silent land barren bereft
Where are the young ones?
Sturdy firm in limb to heave the plough,
To echo happy laughter through the trees?
Dull my eyes maundering dreams of past delights
O how I writhe with moans for a generation never born
To unction eyes and hands to clasp
As body stills and spirit leaps to God
Home in safekeeping will we find them there?
Sweet innocents playing with Angels singing! Praising!
Dancing! Enveloped in love
The land darkens and a deep mist prevails
The few remain to stand upon the shore.
Seeking.

Marie Keown

. . .

HOLD ON GOD—I'LL BE WITH YOU SHORTLY!

Hold on God—I'll be with you shortly!
Good morning Lord,
I've resolved to put You first today.
Just a minute, I ought to have a cup of tea,
And I must peek at the headlines.
Perhaps I should just glance at the TV news.

Bother, that's the phone!
Is it coffee time already?
I won't be long Lord,
Then I'll be right with You.

Sorry, I'll have to answer the door,
"Behold! I stand at the door and knock" (Revelation 3:20)

Doreen Horrigan

FOR REFLECTION

1. Have you already confronted your own shadows?
2. Who are the lepers in your life? How can you conquer your fear of them?
3. What do you still need to embrace both within yourself and in the world around you?

SUGGESTED SCRIPTURE

Mark 10:17–22
Luke 7:36–50; 10:25–37; 16:19–31; 22:60–62

NOTES

[1] Bonaventure, "The Major Legend of Saint Francis" in *Francis of Assisi, Early Documents,* volume II, *The Founder,* Regis J. Armstrong, J.A. Wayne Hellmann, and William J. Short, eds. (New York: New City, 2000), pp. 533–534. Hereafter this volume will be referred to as *FA:ED II* followed by page numbers.

[2] Francis of Assisi, "The Testament," in *Francis and Clare the Complete Works,* Regis J. Armstrong and Ignatius C. Brady, trans. and intro. (New York: Paulist, 1982), p. 154.

[3] *FA:ED II,* "Legend of the Three Companions," p. 74.

THIS STATION DESCRIBES CERTAIN SIGNS THROUGH WHICH FRANCIS BEGAN TO discern the will of God more clearly.

In the early period of his conversion, Francis had dreams and heard voices. His impulsive nature meant that he reacted immediately to these. His spontaneous enthusiasm and urge toward action tended to override a more considered discernment that waits on confirmation. He had not yet learned to truly wait upon the Lord.

Francis was still attracted to knighthood as a noble calling and a way of serving God. He set out to train as a knight under the renowned Walter of Brienne, in Apulia.

Francis had made preparations with characteristic fervor and became ecstatic over a dream, which, he believed, confirmed that he was indeed to be a famous knight. He had dreamed that his home was filled with all sorts of military trappings instead of the usual bales of cloth. However, after this dream, he was surprisingly reluctant when it came to setting forth.

According to the "Legend of the Three Companions," Francis had two dreams. In the first he was brought to the beautiful palace of a wonderful bride where he saw the walls bedecked with military accoutrements. He was amazed to discover that the palace belonged to him and his knights. Thinking that the dream was a directive from God, he immediately set forth and reached Spoleto where he became ill. Resting in that state between sleep and wakefulness, he heard someone ask him who could do him more good—the lord or the servant. Francis retorted "The Lord." The voice challenged him to explain why he was abandoning the Lord for the servant. Francis desperately wanted to know what he had to do. He was told to return to Assisi and await further instruction. He knew that he had not understood the first dream.

Francis reflected on what had occurred and decided to go back to Assisi. His father was bound to be furious, having spent unstintingly to equip his son for knighthood and glory. It was highly probable that Francis would be accused of cowardice and face cruel scorn.

But then Francis received another important sign, according to the "Legend of the Three Companions." While passing by the church of San Damiano, he heard a voice telling him to go inside and pray. While there, he prayed before the now famous San Damiano cross, which he believed talked to him and told him to go and rebuild the church. Francis thought that Christ was telling him to rebuild the actual physical church—the broken-down and aged San Damiano. It would only be much later that Francis realized what Christ was really asking him to do—to rebuild the entire spirit of the church. Nevertheless, Francis was filled with such joy and became so radiant with light over that message that he knew in his soul that it was truly Christ crucified who spoke to him.

He immediately gave money to the priest at San Damiano to buy oil, so that the lamp before the crucifix could be kept burning. He set about making preparations for the restoration work. He hastened to Foligno to sell his horse and some of his father's cloth. On his return, he revealed his conduct to the priest at San Damiano and gave him the money he had secured. The wise priest was somewhat suspicious of this wayward son of the wealthy Pietro Bernardino and declined the money, which the legends tell us Francis threw onto a windowsill.

Pietro had not abandoned his hope that Francis would return to his senses and go back to the family business. He decided the time had come to force the issue. He sent for his son, who promptly went into hiding. According to the *First Life*, Francis spent a month in prayer and fasting. During this period of retreat, Francis learned to hand the situation over to God and no longer rely on his own resources. This led to an indescribable happiness and, fired by God's love, Francis found the strength to face his father's wrath.

His return caused great friction. His father imprisoned him at home and subjected him to beatings. The loving support of his mother, Pica, never wavered. She released Francis from captivity as soon as Pietro set out on his travels, and Francis returned to his work at San Damiano.

When he came home to discover that Francis had been freed, Pietro unleashed his fury on Pica before calling upon the authorities for help. He may have hoped that such public and drastic action would finally bring his son to his senses.

According to the "Legend of the Three Companions," Pietro approached the civil magistrates, wanting them to charge Francis with theft. San Damiano belonged to the church, so anyone working there was subject to ecclesial, not civil, law. Pietro brought his son before Bishop Guido II.

CONTRIBUTIONS

FIERY GOD

Fiery God,
We come to know you in so many diverse ways.
You never cease coming where and when
   we don't expect.
You surprise us in ways
    that delight, that frighten.
 On our journey,
   a journey we choose,
yet which chooses us,
   we yearn and long, and often
   fail to recognize
   our real longing.
We struggle to put on Your mind,
   to choose as you would choose,
   to move beyond recognition and status,
   to be willing to wait, and to wait in darkness.
God of the journey, cleanse us...for your glory.

Mary Albert

. . .

A PRAYER TO THE HOLY SPIRIT FOR THE GRACE TO FOLLOW JESUS MORE CLOSELY

Holy Spirit, Comforter, Counselor, Companion and Friend,
I ask you for the grace to walk always in fellowship with you,
To walk with you as my guide and constant companion.

You who are the breath of God our loving Father,
Help me to conspire with you,
that I may truly and in all sincerity
become a disciple of our beloved Jesus
and live the life of the kingdom of God,
after the example of blessed Francis of Assisi
and all the saints who walked so closely with you.
Amen.

Michael Hagger

. . .

GOD'S CHOOSING

When it was time for you to come
to the earth
your Father chose a teenage girl
untried, inexperienced and afraid,
to be your mother.
Joseph too, to bring you up,
a carpenter, not rich or famous,
living in a small town,
making the everyday things
that people use—
It is strange how God chooses
the ones we would not choose
to do his work.

You were born in a stable
with the animals.
dirty and unhygienic.

No medical facilities
no doctor standing by.
But probably warm from the animals
and plenty of straw about
soft, but rather scratchy,
were there mice?—
It is strange how God chooses
places we would not choose
to come to.

People came to see you.
Shepherds down from the hills
smelling of sheep,
their shoes muddy.
They said that angels had told them
to leave all their sheep in the fields
hoping they would not wander
too far away.
And forgetting the wolves and bears
which might attack and eat them
and to go straight to Bethlehem,
and to find you—
It is strange how God chooses
people we would not choose
to visit you.

Then the Magi came traveling
with their gold, incense and myrrh,
strangers from the eastern lands
from a country we do not know,
with strange clothes and language.

They looked in the palace
but you were not there,
so they followed the star to the stable
and found you,
gave you their gifts,
and worshipped you there
It is strange how God chooses
people we would not choose
to worship you.

God chooses the unexpected
The reluctant, the scared,
the totally flabbergasted.
and those who think they will fail.
He chooses those who seek him,
and those who try to hide;
he chooses the rich and famous
as well as you and me
I am glad that he did the calling
When he wanted the work to be done
because if I had been doing the choosing
would I really have chosen me?

Jill Boal

Lord, be with us this day, in every moment

Lord, be with us this day, in every moment—
in a world gone crazy—you are our peace
in the midst of confusion—you are our certainty, the direction we
seek
in the big moments of this day—you are our gentleness
in the small moments of this day—you are our strength and all that
we need
in the moments of success—you are our prize
in the moments of failure—you are our shepherd
Jesus Lord, breathe your Holy Spirit into our hearts and minds
today—
that we might be your voice
that we might be your hands
that we may love as you do, everyone that we meet this day.
Jesus Lord, at the end of this day,
when the busyness ceases and when our work is done,
May we thank you for today and then,
rest in you, and know
that your will has been done.
Amen.

Margaret Donald

TWO DREAMS

One night I dreamt I was out walking when I saw a robe-clad man coming toward me. I ran to greet him and saw it was Saint Francis. We put our arms around each other in joy. He gave me a strong "Franciscan Hug." As we walked together in fond embrace I saw a huge hill with a cross upon it. We continued to walk toward it with joy.

Another night I dreamt I was lying down wearing my full Franciscan habit. I looked overhead and saw Saint Francis. I reached up for his hands and kissed them. He then placed a white scarf over my eyes to the back of my head. He then proceeded to do the same to someone lying down horizontally at my feet while I was in a vertical position forming a Tau cross.

Waking up I remembered thinking what does it all mean? These two dreams I was graced with?

Two weeks later I was rushed to the hospital where I was given a blood platelet transfusion.

I felt good and happy and at peace all the four days I spent in the hospital.

Coming home and after seeing so much suffering and sickness I prayed to Saint Francis. I then picked up the *Omnibus,* and read 1 Celano on the miracles of Saint Francis.

I started to think of all the sufferings and sickness in my family; my husband with a cancer history of twenty-seven years, my own medical problems and now we find my son diagnosed with multiple sclerosis. He is forty-four years old.

Remembering my dreams I realized that Saint Francis was with me and interceded for me and made me well. I was then inspired to write the following prayer:

A Prayer to Saint Francis for Healing

O holy Saint Francis, most joyful of all Saints, your love for God and His church made you worthy, when on earth, to be the founder of your three orders. So filled with the love of God, your joy and hope caused others to follow your way in following Our Lord by living the Holy Gospel. I implore you, for the love of God, to obtain a healing cure for (name). As you kissed the leper, please kiss this illness and bring it to an end, not only for (name) but for all who suffer from it. O loving Saint Francis, whisper this petition to the baby Jesus in the crèche and to Jesus on the San Damiano Cross. As He spoke to you, speak now to Jesus and the gratitude of my heart will be yours forever.

Thank you Saint Francis. Pray for us.

Teresa Ascione

. . .

Hope

Flocks of birds, in medieval times, symbolized crowds of common people.
Saint Francis did preach to the birds, but more important,
he gave the common people the message that they were
"Buona gente," good people loved by God.
His message for them and for us is to believe in our own self-worth
and to face life with courage and hope.

Mary Esther Stewart

FOR REFLECTION

1. You may ask God for clear signposts, but we need the eyes to see and the ears to hear so we can recognize them. Do you let others help you in your discernment process?
2. Do you believe that God is really concerned about what you do?

SUGGESTED SCRIPTURE

Matthew 6:8–13; 7:21
John 4:1–38
Romans 7:14–20
Philippians 2:13

STATION FIVE: THE BISHOP'S PALACE

AT THIS STATION, FRANCIS DENOUNCES HIS FATHER, PIETRO BERNARDONE, strips himself naked, returns everything he possesses to his father and hands himself over to the bishop. This station marks a clearer turning from past ties in Francis' life. He has exhausted his father's patience, and they part ways. In a dramatic and final gesture in front of a crowd of people, Francis throws his clothes back in his father's face and rejects him. The event sends a shockwave throughout the whole city. It is not hard to imagine the reactions that echo through the crowd gathered for this curious trial. Francis' conversion, with its radical consequences, was no longer a private matter.

In Saint Bonaventure's recollection of the event, he draws attention to the roughness of the clothing Francis immediately dons after his conversion. The crowd must have been struck by the contrast with the elegant and fashionable costumes of his past. Francis marked his new tunic with the sign of the cross, and thereafter was identified as a *penitent*, part of a recognized order of Christians. These men and women sought, as individuals, to live a gospel life, following the poor and naked Christ.

Pietro had been a good and loving father and some people have reflected that Francis' earthly father provided a positive role model. The relationship between Francis and his father was a good foundation for the intimate relationship that Francis would eventually build with his father in heaven. Paradoxically, his earthly father had finally "presented" Francis to his new mother, the church.

For Francis and Clare, stripping off attachments formed in early life meant completely overturning their former lives. For the communities they were to form, living *sine proprio*, without appropriating anything to oneself, would become a benchmark of gospel life. Near the end of his life, Francis wrote the following in the "Letter to the Entire Order": "Hold back nothing of yourselves for yourselves, / that He who gives Himself totally to you /may receive you totally."[1]

Contributions

FRANCIS

Francis
Before the church-clothed Bishop, you stood—
self-dispossessed
And with you, coming not late, your bethrothed,
Lady Poverty
And many there, saw not her face nor her beauty,
but mistook
Thinking her fine apparel rags, they mocked, hurled
bouquets of mud
Yet the union blessed; together went out, an idiot and
his lady, jubilating ...
such songs that the air and the wind; the birds and the wolf—danced
your Master's praise

Other ears opening to these two voices singing—one love,
one life
born from a broken tree—heard most true the bass notes
of the Word
of their making, "Come, come now to the banquet, but

not alone

bring—the threadbare, the ones in your time made lepers,

those condemned...

for the feasting in the Kingdom continues...still there are empty

places at the table

where Lady Poverty presides having woven wedding garments fit

for the meal; enough

for each of us who enter through the door, with our rich life poor,

our bitter wounds

Put upon us—this garb shall burst into Brother Fire, warming the
     heart

to share in your joy.

Kathryn Hamaan

.   .   .

PIAZZA DEL VESCOVADO

Oh God, how could he do it?

I stand at the door of our guest house, looking into the courtyard of the bishop's palace, and wonder about the conflict and stresses which drove Francis to strip himself naked and hand back everything he possessed to his father.

Was he ever reconciled with Pietro Bernardone? Or at least with his mother? There is nothing to suggest it, but I feel they must have met again in the narrow, winding streets of Assisi. Surely he would not have passed Donna Pica without embracing her?

Family breakdown is nothing new. I feel challenged to pray more for my own family, and for the families in my church. What stresses are they facing? Are the teenagers rebelling against parental control? Can I help in any way by my friendship and support?

I think of the church of St. Nicholas, which stood near here, where Francis opened the Gospels to learn God's will for his life. He realized that his Lord was speaking directly to him through the words he read:

Sell all that you have and give to the poor.

Take nothing for your journey.

Deny yourself, take up your cross and follow me.

Joyfully he cried out to his two companions, Bernard and Giles, "Brothers, this is our life and rule, for ourselves and for all who will join our company."

Now I am asking to join that same company, as I look forward to profession in the Secular Franciscans. I too want to respond joyfully and wholeheartedly as the Lord speaks to me through Scripture.

Oh God, how can I do it?

I cannot sell everything I have, but I could give far, far more to help the poor and disadvantaged in the world. I cannot take nothing for my journey, but I am challenged to free myself from the ties of property and possessions, to live simply in the spirit of Saint Francis.

"Deny yourself," says the Lord. "Follow me." I don't know where he will lead me, what joys or disappointments I may experience along the way, what challenges I may meet.

Oh God, how can I do it?

Slowly I turn back from the street and walk through to the tranquil garden of the guest house. I take out my pen and a sheet of paper, and settle down to write my personal Rule as an Anglican Tertiary.

It was here that Francis turned his back on everything that the world holds dear, to follow only his Lord. Oh God, help me to do the same.

Ann Leigh

What's in a Word?

To "surrender" to you, Lord, sounds like
an army on the losing side,
   even though to surrender to you is
to win everything that has meaning on this side of heaven—or the
next.
   To "surrender" to you, Lord, sounds like
a laying down of arms, a negotiated treaty,
   even though a surrender to you is
to receive a limitless
unconditional love.
   Ah! But to "abandon" oneself to you sounds like
to leap the great divide from here
to Love on the Cross.
   Sounds like to leave everything behind
name, gender, possessions,
all that makes "me" mine
   And to be set on fire with such a passion
that only a rare being like Saint Francis
shows us a glimmer of what could be.
   No, Lord, "surrender" is not in our vocabulary.
But as you call "Come" and Love rises from the Cross
With every particle of the "me" that You made long ago
   I leap—and melt into
     An endless
       Kaleidoscope of
    color and harmony and laughter of delight
    Whirling into space
     With all those
     Who were and are and are to come.

> Totus tuus, totus tuus
Totally yours
For ever and ever and ever and ever and...

Sheila Brayford

. . .

ACCORDING TO THY WORD

Poverty is that stillness of soul
Which leans on nothing but the presence of God,
Only God, yet all besides
To him who is poor.
Listen to poverty, that clear ringing Of the
Angelus bell which calls to the simplicity
Of poverty's prayer: Be it done unto me
According to Thy word.
From man's poverty, perceived and accepted,
Springs All, as infinite God
Seizes selflessness for His greatest
Creative Act.
O miracle, that takes creature's nothingness
For its most colossal ends.
O bewilderment, fill my soul
With awe,
Deep-plunging, heart-cold awe,
For I my God have seen
And Heaven-chosen poverty know
As God's own choice
For God.
Mary, pray that "Fiat!"

May make us poor
Of all save God.

Robina Knewstub

. . .

THANK YOU FATHER FOR ALL CREATION

Thank you Father for all creation. I know that You are saving the whole world. May I participate in whatever way it is Your Will that I participate. I know that I will have to offer up sacrifices of time and money for Your purpose. And I am willing to do that, because I also want everyone to go to heaven. I also don't want anyone to say no to You Almighty and Eternal Father. I pray that the Holy Spirit will enlighten me as to how I might best fulfill Your plan for my life. I ask this in Jesus' name. Amen.

Beverly Schmerse

FOR REFLECTION

1. Try to become aware of interior attachments, attachment to emotions like anger or jealousy.

2. Think of an achievement you have accomplished and a gift that you have. In prayer, return these to God from whom all that is good in you has come.

SUGGESTED SCRIPTURE

Mark 15:16–20

Luke 12:22–34; 19:18–30

Philippians 2:5–11

NOTE
[1] *FA:ED I,* "A Letter to the Entire Order," p. 118.

STATION SIX: THE HERALD OF THE GREAT KING

THIS STATION IS SET IN LATE WINTER, ON A TRACK NEAR ASSISI. FRANCIS HAD previously left Assisi in search of knighthood. That would have brought glory to his family and the city. After renouncing his father and abandoning family ties, with the blessing of the bishop, he set out in the direction of Gubbio. This time he was dressed as a penitent, wearing a cross, the insignia of his Lord. It was cold. There was still some snow on the ground.

Francis traveled light, carrying nothing of value. A band of robbers noticed him and decided to have some sport. They started to taunt him. When they asked him who he was, he said that he was the herald of the great King. This provoked them into beating the fool, and throwing him into a ditch, filled with snow. Feeling curiously overjoyed and liberated, the "herald" got up, shook off the snow, and continued on his way, proclaiming his Lord with songs of praise.[1]

He spent a few days serving as a scullery boy in a monastery but, "No mercy was shown him and he was not even able to get some old clothes." [2] He arrived at Gubbio where he met a friend who greeted him warmly and gave him a cheap tunic. He was now dressed as a hermit. Francis decided to return to the area around Assisi. He served the poor and needy, spending some time at a leper hospital, probably either San Rufino dell'Arce or San Lazaro.[3]

He continued to carry out building work on little churches in and around Assisi. He discovered the remains of a church dedicated to the Blessed Mother, called the Portiuncula. Celano informs us that:

At that time it was deserted and no one was taking care of it. When the holy man of God saw it so ruined, he was moved by piety because he had a warm devotion to the Mother of all good and he began to stay there continually. The restoration of that church took place in the third year of his conversion. [4]

On the feast of Saint Matthias, February 24, 1208, Francis paid particular attention to the Gospel of the day, which was the commissioning of the disciples. Jesus instructed them to travel in pairs, preaching penance and proclaiming the kingdom of God. They were to travel without gold, silver or money, without a wallet, a sack, bread or a staff, wearing neither shoes nor a tunic. After Mass, Francis asked the priest to explain it fully to him.[5] He rejoiced that he at last had found clear direction. With all of his heart and soul, he desired to live the evangelical life faithfully.

Celano tells us that Francis changed his habit once more—into a cross-shaped tunic made out of rough cloth, with a cord instead of a leather belt. He was to proclaim the good news of Christ, his Lord. Then others would share his happiness and certainty of God's love that, as he had discovered, transformed everything. He was indeed a herald of the great king.

CONTRIBUTIONS

GOD KNOCKS—OPEN MY HEART

"God enters by a private door into every individual."

—Ralph Waldo Emerson

Let us vision a man tall, slender whose image is the Son of man.

He comes to the door and knocks. Will we open the door to let Him in?

Will we choose to keep the door shut?

Who is He? The man, is He any man? Can He be trusted with such a gift?

Is He at the right door? Is He at the right place?

The man approaches as to a child unknowing—the child will let everyone come in.

We as children are so generous; we have learned to show love.

He then approaches as to an adult, we are reserved. We question, who are you?

We have doubts, we have fears, and some will open the door, some will not.

The Son of man knocks on the door of our hearts every day.

He wants to know if we will be open to His whispers, and His touch.

He wants to touch our Soul, our heart and our mind.

We have to remain as children in order for Him to enter us and then, Bring us to His Kingdom and His Love.

Susan Daneault, S.F.O.

Living Life

You gave me life
  Almighty God.

I give it back to You.
Do with it what You will.
My life, while mine, is Yours.

  Accept my offering—though small.
'Tis all I have
'Tis what you gave
Let me return it full.

Jean Bloomer

. . .

Francis Once Took a Certain Sick Brother

In "The Second Life of Saint Francis," Thomas Celano writes about how Francis took a sick brother, who Francis knew to be longing for grapes, into a vineyard and first ate the grapes to give the sick man the courage to eat. Francis sat down with the brother and ate. He did not send a representative, or just the grapes or a note to the sick friar. Francis found some bread and fruit and sat on the ground with the hungry friar. He said nothing but simply began eating with the friar. Francis gave the gift of his presence to his friar. He gave the gift of being there.

So, I will call my friend or family and just say, "I am with you." I will visit them with a bowl of grapes or a piece of good bread and bowl of soup. I will eat with them and sit with them and offer my humble gift of presence and support. That is all I can give. I will be a living card by my being there.

Just like the gospel message, "simple, but hard to live out" my presence to others will be my gift of time, that part of my daily life which I guard for things which are important, sacred. Prayer is the ultimate gift of God's presence. Our presence with each other will be our healing prayer. We have to be there with each other to receive that presence. It will be a time of prayer for us both. We have to be there. Our gift in times of poor health is being there.

Karen Zielinski

. . .

POETIC PROFILE

Irene, in Greek, means "PEACE"
October 1 is my feast—
Birth Anniversary and Children's Day it is—
Will always remind me to be a child of Peace!

At the age of twelve I heard a call,
Then I prayed to God, Who is my All—
Vividly that night, I can recall,
And my thirst for Him grew more and more.
Eight years of search and yearning, before
my baptism as a Child of God.
In body and soul I was restored

On November 18, 1978 I recall.
A beautiful name I have for my Profession
Mary Frances, was what I had chosen.
It took me a long time to discern—
Finally to be a Franciscan—is my vocation!
In 1988 I joined the S.F.O.

Two years of formation I had to undergo.
A Formator for the fraternity—I was told
At the Election, the votes would show.
A difficult task for me to carry
Like Jesus, it is the road to Calvary.
Shouldering this responsibility
Is definitely not so easy!
Sourcing for talents in the fraternity
Besides "forming" the Secular Franciscans to be!
Part of the Formator's responsibility
Is also to make new discovery.

The Holy Eucharist I would receive frequently
In the Cenacle encountering God almost daily—
This is part of our Franciscan Spirituality
Is to tread the path of Saint Francis more closely.

To do the Will of the Father is my one goal,
In all the things I do with heart and soul.
To reap the harvest for what I have sown
Thus fulfilling my commitment to the S.F.O.

Coming from a large Taoist family
The Gospel way of life is a challenge for me.
Achieving sainthood is top priority—
Ultimately to reach Heaven is my destiny!

My profession as a Secretary
Presently serving in the Singapore Archdiocese.
To be a Franciscan there is not easy—
There are many struggles to overcome daily.

My Chinese name speaks loud
In unity with the creation of God, I found
Sister Water, Brother Sun, and Sister Moon are what it holds,
Now the meaning of it, is unfold!
Inculturation with Franciscan Spirituality
Is, my name another discovery...

In a talk by a Franciscan Missionary
On Francis and Ecology!
A strong character I possess
Aggressiveness is what I detest!
Becoming a saint I have yet—
Is to pray to God, the All-Perfect.
"Punching" Francis is my hobby!
Besides knitting Humpty-Dumptys!
Making use of the talent of Father Kevin
To draw Friar Snoopy for me!

Photograph I have none at hand
Seeing is believing—one would understand
The Creator made me beautiful by His hand—
The Artist! Who would dare to offend?
The story of Irene thus ends here—
I hope Christ's values grow year by year,
As support and guidance given by my peers
In following Francis, I have no fears.

Irene Ang

The Call

The call didn't come from a leper or even a talking crucifix.

There aren't a lot of those in Pennsylvania.

Instead, a small paragraph in a small newspaper.

God has no hands but ours.

A thousand reasons not to go.

Trying hard "to avoid the divine grasp."

The rush of emotion

The tears of fright.

The pain of trusting.

The Lord showed me "what I must do."

A place to be who I was called to be.

"This is why every order, sex, and age finds in Francis

a clear pattern of the teaching of salvation

and an outstanding example of holy deeds."

Every day, a new struggle.

Always, a new commitment.

"Twenty years have now passed since the conversion."

Marie Clardy

. . .

Everyone Has a Key

The old friar lay in his cell waiting to greet Sister Death. For more years than anyone could remember, he had been "Brother Tailor." He had made the habits for countless brothers. Then mended them year after year. And vestments for divine services tailored by him were used in churches far and wide. Now he was so weak that his voice was little more than a whisper. Father Guardian put his ear close to the old brother's mouth to hear him better.

"He's asking for his 'key to heaven,'" Father frowned. "Does anyone know what he means?"

"I'll get his rosary," one of the friars offered.

Within minutes, the rosary was placed in the dying man's hands. Feebly he shook his head and asked again for his key to heaven.

"Perhaps he wants his prayer book," suggested another.

He returned with the well-worn prayer book, but it met with no more success than the rosary. Still came the whispered plea for his key to heaven.

For a few awkward minutes, no one knew what to do. Then a young novice suddenly brightened.

"I think I know," he said. Quickly but very quietly, he left. Soon the panting novice returned holding, of all things, a needle.

"Here, Brother Tailor. Here is your key to heaven." He knelt beside the bed and offered the needle.

A faint smile lit the old face; wrinkled fingers took the needle and lifted it to dry colorless lips.

You see, Brother Tailor had done more with that needle than pull thread through cloth. He had prayed with it. Every stitch had been an act of service to others, and to God. Truly, his needle was his key to heaven.

Each of us has a key to heaven. What's yours? The steering wheel of a truck? The slide rule of an engineer? The trowel of a bricklayer? The apron of a housewife? The scalpel of a surgeon? The law books of a solicitor? Or the muscle and sweat of a laborer? Whatever it is, use it in loving service to others, for the love of God, and it will open heaven's doors for you just as smoothly as Brother Tailor's needle did for him.

Every one of us has his own individual key. And perhaps everyone has his own individual stigmata. Saint Francis of Assisi and a few others were chosen to have the visible marks of Christ's wounds in their own bodies. This was, as it was made clear to Francis, for the edification of others more than for the stigmatists themselves. But we are all expected to "take up our cross" and follow Jesus. We are all called to share in his tremendous struggle and in his final victory over evils. Everyone who accepts the challenge to carry the cross of Christ is a private stigmatist.

What is your stigmata? A wayward child? A quarrelsome husband? Drug dependency? Financial burdens? Fits of despondency or loneliness? An incurable disease?

For the sake of others, we must try to "cure" some of these stigmata. But, while they exist, don't waste them. Perhaps no one else will ever see your wounds as Brother Leo saw the bleeding wounds of Francis. But Jesus will see them. He will see your bleeding heart and He will know that you are helping Him carry His cross.

And Mary will see them. And that most loving, most caring of all mothers will say, "Jesus, he needs help to carry that cross," just as she once said, "Jesus, they have no wine." And her prayer will not go unheard.

Lee Lampe

. . .

A Child's Prayer

Francis and Clare
You showed God such love
Living humbly here
Living only for God
Hear now our prayer
That we might also love too

And live out our lives
Following Jesus like you.

Elizabeth Cornwell

.   .   .

Brother Wind

In our parish a few of the Sunday Masses are celebrated in an auditorium next door to the church. After the last Mass, any extra consecrated hosts are reverently carried back to the tabernacle in the church.

Recently, a very young new priest learned the hard way about the startling gusts of wind that sometimes sneak between the two buildings, even during summer.

The covers on the two Communion plates that he was so carefully carrying back to the church were suddenly swept off and dozens of consecrated hosts went swirling through the air like sanctified snowflakes. I shall never forget Father's anguish as I ran to his aid. Hosts were everywhere, on the pavement, the lawn, and in the shrubbery, we spent considerable time on our hands and knees searching prayerfully for each of them,

As I poked under some perky geraniums, an answer in the long ago the *Baltimore Catechism* came to mind, "God is everywhere!"

Somehow, a smile broke through the sacred seriousness of the situation. It was as if I was given a surprise gift. Earlier I had been distracted during Mass, and now a very patient Jesus was delaying my return home in order to correct that He certainly caught my full attention!

Could He be calling after me for a forgotten farewell hug? Gently I felt, rather than heard, His question, "Isn't there something you forgot to tell me during Holy Communion?"

There sure was!

When I finished my belated prayer, and He was safely back in His tabernacle, I begged Him, "Oh please Jesus, tell brother Francis for me, how deeply I too treasure his friend, Brother Wind."

Claire Campbell

. . .

Do You Know How Important You Are?

You may be the only way someone could see God! You could change the path one takes with just an understanding nod.
A despairing spirit might need a lift.
Your words might do the trick.
You can bring the peace of Christ
to someone who's heartsick.
You might just need to listen—
and never say a word. (Even though you're silent, your caring will be heard!)
It might require a smile or hug:
maybe a pat on the back.
You can show them they are good
and give them what they lack.

It may be that they truly doubt
The good they have inside. Their life might be tough right now, and they've lost their inner guide.
They may be needing assurance
That God hasn't moved away.
Be ready to share your faith with them.
It might just make their day!

I KNOW HOW IMPORTANT YOU ARE!

(and I hope you know it too)

Because you see, you've changed my life—

Just by being you!

It's amazing what wonderful things happen

When faith, hope and love blend.

I thank you for so much caring

And especially for being my friend.

Valerie Cadarr

. . .

TO TRIUNE GOD AFTER RECEIVING EUCHARIST

God my creator

Breathe on me again

Renew me—Refresh me

Extend my abilities

Body and Blood of Jesus Christ

Flow through every fiber of my being

Keep me well

Oh Holy Spirit use me.

Mary Smith

A CHILD'S POEM

Lord, help me to know the talent you've given me,
So I can make it grow, to share with those I see.
Lord, help me to know the talent you've given me,
So I can make it grow, the better steward be.
Lord, help me to know the talent you've given me,
So I can make it grow, and have You proud of me.

Ron Madison

. . .

LORD, MAKE ME AN INSTRUMENT OF YOUR PEACE

Since the beginning of Creation, and even to our present time, to forgive and be forgiven is a need we all experience. To every home, every office, community and country, the cry for peace and forgiveness is universal.

In my own little way, I want to share how the Lord God had inspired me through the Peace Prayer attributed to Saint Francis of Assisi. I have tried this personally and to a few friends I have already shared.

In the early beginnings of my religious formation in the monastery, I encountered some difficult situations which naturally involved persons. It then dawned on me that difficult situations were somehow helps or bridges one has to cross as part of one's inner journey to God.

Eventually, in my silent struggle, the Lord, I daresay, had personally taught me an aid to hold on to the railings of faith and conscious effort to go forward in spite of difficulties. The recitation of this Peace Prayer which our community recited daily and communally, after every eucharistic celebration, had immeasurable influence on me. Somehow the message of the Peace Prayer slowly sank into my subconscious and became part of my being. Without knowing when and how it started, a method on forgiving simply came to my mind.

This is it:

> During the singing or recitation of the Our Father in the Divine Office and most especially during eucharistic celebrations, I silently and sincerely insert the name of the particular person that I need to forgive or that needed to forgive me. After the phrase, forgive us our trespasses as we forgive.... I attentively insert the name of the person. I continually repeat this practice. Then the time just comes when I already feel that I no longer have to do it for I already feel peace in my heart with regard to this person, however near or far from me physically. I may not have forgotten what and how the incident happened, but my reaction is no longer pain or anger or whatever negative emotion used to follow each time it was remembered. I have attained the peace my heart desires. Then later, at any time of the day or night that I pray, I continue to praise God and sincerely bless the person concerned. The kind of peace which I experience is coupled with inner joy which truly as the Lord said, only He can bestow. Thanks to Saint Francis of Assisi who is widely known as a man of peace and reconciler of those in discord. Thanks to whoever it was who composed the Peace Prayer which served as inspiration to thousands or millions of people in the world in much need of healing particularly in relationships. Above all, I praise and give glory to God who deemed it worthy for His poor Saint Francis to be an instrument of peace.

Mary Veronica Ceniza, O.S.C.

Vocation

Lines to our Holy Father Saint Francis
Traces of your presence
I encountered at each turning;
Bittersweet caresses
Thrilled my young heart's yearning.

Your Seraphic shadow
Haunted every dream I spun me;
But it was your wistful smile
That won me.

Sister Eileen Lillis

. . .

God Called to Me

God called to me in the
Springtime of my life,
In a field of snowdrops,
As I mended a broken doll,
At my first ballet lesson,
During the Sunday school picnic,
When I saw a newborn calf,
And on the day my younger brother died.

God called to me in the
Summertime of my life,
On my "Gap-Year" travels,
When I sailed the oceans,
Joined in wedlock,
Gave birth to my children,

Bought my first house,
And as I scaled the career ladder.

God called to me in the
Autumn time of my life,
As I sang in the church choir,
Supported my children,
Cultivated an allotment,
Contemplated retirement,
Grappled with new technology,
And buried my parents.

God called to me in the
Wintertime of my life,
When I became a grandparent,
Managed on a pension,
Moved to sheltered accommodation,
Through the pain of my illness,
And when I lost my hearing aid.
God called to me...and I listen well.

Margaret Boden-Heaume

For Reflection

Spend time reflecting on how faithfully you are living out your life.

Suggested Scripture

1 Samuel 3:1–10
The book of Jonah
Luke 5:1–11

NOTES
[1] *FA:ED I*, "The Life of Saint Francis," p. 194.
[2] *FA:ED I*, "The Life of Saint Francis," p. 195.
[3] Information about lepers can be found in Arnaldo Fortini, *Francis of Assisi*, Helen Moak, trans. (New York: Crossroad), pp. 260ff.
[4] *FA:ED I*, "The Life of Saint Francis," p. 201.

STATION SEVEN: RIVO TORTO

THIS STATION MARKS THE BEGINNING OF THE FRANCISCAN MOVEMENT. Francis and his companions traveled to Rome where they secured the approval of Pope Innocent III to persevere in their way of following the gospel life. The legends tell us that the little community stayed in a tiny hut at Rivo Torto on their return. They were evicted by a pig farmer who wanted shelter for his animals.[1]

The community began to form after Francis had started preaching in Assisi and his way of life and commitment caught the imagination of other young citizens, including Bernard of Quintavalle, a lawyer. The story about Bernard inviting Francis to dine and stay with him overnight is celebrated in the Franciscan tradition. Both men pretended to be asleep. Francis got up to spend the night in prayer and Bernard secretly watched him. This convinced Bernard that Francis was serious and genuine, not crazy. Having satisfied any doubts, he asked Francis if he could join him.

Seeking inspiration, the two companions went to the church of St. Nicholas in Assisi to consult the Gospels. Their eyes fell on the following Scripture:

> If you wish to be perfect, go, sell your possessions and give the money to the poor, and you will have treasure in heaven; then come, follow me. (Matthew 19:21)

> Take nothing for the journey, nor staff, nor bag, nor bread, nor money—not even an extra tunic. (Luke 9:3)

If any want to become my followers, let them deny themselves and take up their cross and follow me. (Matthew
16:24)

This was to be their life, based on the evangelical life of the disciples
in the early church. As Francis stated it in his *Testament*, "And after
the Lord gave me brothers, no one showed me what I should do, but
the Most High Himself revealed to me that I should live according to
the form of the Holy Gospel."[2]

As a result of the decision to follow these passages literally, no one
could be accepted into the company until they had sold all their possessions. Francis directed their formation as the companions explored
their faith together, discussing their way of life along the way.[3]

Once there were eight companions, they followed the missionary
journeys of the disciples and went out in pairs, each pair taking a different direction. A pattern was established of preaching, initially
within Italy, and returning to meet together at the Portiuncula for
"chapters."

Francis, with twelve companions, traveled to Rome to meet the
pope, seeking approval for their proposed way of life. This was about
the year 1209. With the assistance and advice of churchmen, he
secured an audience with the pope, who gave oral approval to their
proposal.[4] Francis was granted authority to preach penance and he
and his followers received the tonsure, an outward sign of this permission. [5]

Soon after, Francis had approached first Bishop Guido and the
canons of San Rufino for a place for shelter, but there was no place
for Francis and his companions. The Benedictine monks on Mount
Subasio gave them permission to use their little church. Francis
insisted on some "rent" to prevent claiming rights of ownership over
their new home. It was agreed that Francis would give the monks an

amount of fish every year on the feast of Saint Benedict, and the monks would provide a jar of oil for the brothers.

CONTRIBUTIONS

POVERELLO

Little Brother, quietly standing
At the turning of our lives, Gently loving, humbly giving,
Christ in us to realize;
Through the centuries you have called us,
Across the barriers of time and space,
Come my brothers, come my sisters
The Lord will fill us with his Grace.

Graham Tyler

. . .

FRANCIS

Wild youth of Assisi,
Disturber of the peace,
Until the Lady Poverty,
Saw your carousing cease.

Little Brother, Francis,
The friend of wolf and hare.
Preacher to the songbirds
And laying Christ's love bare.

God's own fool for Jesus,
Rebuilder of His Church,
See how much we need thee, as
For unity we search.

Father to the Brothers,
And soulmate of Saint Clare,
Inspiration through the years
Of people everywhere.

Founder of the Order,
And pointer to the way
Of treading in Christ's footsteps
Til our ascension day.

Tertiary, West Wales Group

. . .

JESUS, LIGHT OF THE WORLD

Jesus, Sun of Justice, you left your heavenly realm of light
To dwell here, a tiny embryonic spark,
At Mary's "Yes" to God's request through Gabriel.
The unborn John leapt for joy at your shining Presence
When Mary entered Elizabeth's house.

The angels could not contain their exuberant wonder
As they burst into song at your radiant birth.

Your created astral light guided Magi when your
Glowing glory was revealed at Bethlehem's cave
You the light of nations shone out to Simeon
And gleams of wisdom were made manifest
To learned priests in the Temple at Jerusalem.

Loving Lord Jesus, you humbly allowed
Your baptism by John, when holy Love
Shone from you, Father and Spirit.

An unearthly light blazed from you on Tabor
Transfiguring you in gleaming glory.

Your nourishing light of grace came first
At Thursday's Supper, and lovingly, gently
Bathes us at daily Eucharist,
Endlessly enriching and enlightening us,
So that we may take it out and give to others:
So that we may shine with your love to all.

The light of your love conquered death, when
Your glory, revealed in majesty and regal splendor,
Risen, triumphant, yet calm and forgiving shone out.
The darkness of sin no longer dominant in this world:

Your loving light burns away Satan's suggestions
Healing our weak wayward souls and illuminating
The dark recesses of our minds
Showing our meanness and petty failures.

Yet this glorious light strengthens and heals
Helps us to hope, be molded and transformed
Into the light *you* want us to be.
So that we can radiate your love out to all,
Shining, smiling out as you have asked us;
"Let your light shine out to all mankind."

Let us be like Francis and Clare, satellites to your Sun,
Shining moons reflecting your love.
Let us be true Franciscans, glowing wordlessly, silently,
Mirroring your compassion to all:
All your smiling light pouring out from us.

Dear Jesus, let us shine as you shine,
To give your love to all we meet.
All of it will be your light and love
Shining through us, praising, glowing,
To show the way, Your Way...
To show the truth, Your Truth...
To show the indwelling life, Your Life.

Hilary Carter

. . .

VOCATION PRAYER

Loving God,
You gave us our Franciscan vocation; we treasure this gift and we thank You for it.
We pray that we can share this gift with others and, with Francis and Clare, lead them to Your Son.
Holy Spirit of God, be with us. Amen.

Cath Spongberg

FOR REFLECTION

Reflect on your participation in the various communities of which you are a part.

SUGGESTED SCRIPTURE

John 20:19–29

Acts 2:41–47; 6:1–7; 15:1–35

NOTES

[1] *FA:ED I*, "The Life of Saint Francis," pp. 220–223.

[2] Francis of Assisi, "The Testament" 14, in *Francis and Clare the Complete Works*, pp. 154–155.

[3] A study of the "Earlier Rule," in *FA:ED I*, pp. 63–86, gives insight into how the way of life evolved as the brothers experimented and learned what was practical and essential.

[4] *FA:ED I*, "The Life of Saint Francis," p. 205.

[5] At this time there were many itinerant preachers, some of whom spread heretical teachings. The church was anxious to control this trend and was preparing to clamp down on heresy by restricting new groups, while at the same time seeking to prepare the clergy better for their preaching ministry. There was a major council in 1215, Lateran Council IV, which established policies for bringing about these reforms. Francis would have been aware of the need for caution and he wanted to be assured of the approval of the church for the work he was doing.

STATION EIGHT: CLARE'S CALL

In 1193 or 1194, Clare was born into one of the most powerful families in Assisi. Her parents were Ortolana and Favarone di Offreduccio. Their family home was adjacent to the Cathedral of San Rufino, overlooking its piazza.

Favarone and his brothers were distinguished knights. When Clare was very young, civil war broke out and her family fled to Perugia with other members of the nobility. There was ongoing warfare between the papal and imperial states and Europe was involved in the Crusades, so Clare's father was often away. Her mother was renowned for her holiness. She also traveled, on pilgrimages. Clare was generous by nature and used to feed the poor from the family table. She gave money to Francis for the restoration work he was doing on local churches.

As the eldest of three girls, Clare would have been expected to make a good marriage and increase the power and wealth of the family.

Francis made a strong impression upon Clare. She was aware of the gravity of his actions when he renounced his father in front of the bishop. Francis worked in the vicinity of Assisi, so Clare knew how he lived among the outcast.

Clare had no interest in marriage. Living beside the cathedral, she heard Francis preaching and knew that he spent vigils in prayer in the crypt of San Rufino. She was inspired by his words and deeds and wanted to find out more. They met, chaperoned by Lady Bona de Guelfuccio, sometimes in San Rufino, sometimes at San Damiano. Clare also wanted to live the gospel life, humbly, simply and in poverty. She made her permanent commitment to evangelical life when she escaped from her family home to go to the brothers on the night of Palm Sunday, 1212.

At that morning Mass Clare remained in her place in San Rufino and the Bishop came to her to present her with a palm.[1] That night she left her home for the last time. She succeeded in escaping from the securely locked house and made her way to the Portiuncula. Here Francis received her into religious life and tonsured her.

Clare knew that she had wronged her family. Some regarded her actions as shameful. She had already given her dowry away, as she wanted to live in absolute poverty. That night she finally stripped herself of all the trappings of her former life. The tonsure was an irrevocable sign of her new life within the church. She had chosen Jesus as her spouse and that night she became his bride.

Clare could not live among the brothers, traveling from place to place, without security. She had to discern how to live out this new life. Francis and the brothers took her to a Benedictine monastery, San Paolo delle Ancelle di Dio (known as San Paolo delle Abbadesse). Given Clare's social position, everything must have been prearranged.

However, Clare was a misfit. Rich women brought dowries on entering a monastery. Clare had no dowry nor did she have family approval. She wanted to be treated as a poor servant.

She was as unwelcome as Francis had been at the monastery on the way to Gubbio. She had contravened social laws and customs by her flight. Some members of the community might have feared the inevitable reaction from Clare's family. In fact, the monastery became the scene of a struggle between Clare and her relatives, led by her uncle Monaldus. They arrived, fully armed, determined to forcibly remove Clare. However, they retreated in shock once Clare,

gripping the altar with all her might, revealed her tonsure.
Clare could hardly stay at the monastery after causing such com-
motion. Although the brothers had received her on that perfect Palm
Sunday, once she entered the monastery, she was alone.
Only sixteen days after her flight, Francis arrived to take her to the
community at Sant'Angelo di Panzo on Mount Subasio. Fortini has
little good to say about this place:

> Everything there is dry and desolate, the cliff that hangs
> over it, forbidding in appearance and in name—Sasso Cupo
> (dark stone), the parched bed of Rigo Secco (dry stream)
> and the puny olive trees that climb up the stony slope. The
> only living thing in this landscape is the copious spring that
> murmurs, wheedles, and invites with its subdued melody.[2]

Here she was joined by her sister, Catherine, who took the name of
Agnes. This must have given Clare fresh heart and made the family
even more furious. Monaldus led another band of knights, with even
greater determination, prepared to see Catherine killed, rather than
lose another member of the family to this madness. Catherine was
punched and dragged by the hair as they tried to remove her.[3] When
she begged her sister to pray for her, Clare fell prostrate, in earnest
petition and tears.

> Suddenly, in fact [Agnes'] body lying on the ground seemed
> so heavy, many...exerted all their energy and were not able
> to carry her beyond a certain stream...
> Then Lord Monaldus, her enraged uncle, intended to
> strike her a lethal blow; [but] an awful pain suddenly struck
> the hand he had raised and for a long time the anguish of
> pain afflicted it.[4]

Clare asked her relatives to give up the conflict and entrust Catherine (Agnes) to her care. Agnes gave herself to the service of the Lord and Francis tonsured her.

Soon after this, the sisters moved to San Damiano, where Clare founded her community of Poor Ladies and remained until her death in 1253.

The terrifying experience at Sant'Angelo provided absolute confirmation of Clare's call. She and her sister experienced the infinite love and power of God in the miracle that enabled Agnes to stay.

Contributions

San Damiano

San Damiano, hidden in the vines,
Framed in the silver peace of olive groves,
Fragrant with lavender and pungent thyme—
The cradle of our Order, humble, poor,
The hallowed reliquary of our peace.
Each nook and crevice spell the blessed names:
Our Father Francis and our Mother Clare.

A lonely olive mounts a guard of prayer,
And cypresses defy the flow of Time.
This is the home of Lady Poverty
The simple threshold of the courts of God;
His Sacred Presence fills the holy place.
Here spoke the Crucified to him who was
Himself to be a living crucifix:
"Go, Francis, and repair anew My Church,
Which, as you see, is falling to decay."

Here all is purity, serene and strong;
Here all is wrapped in silence and in prayer.
Like that bright flame that rose with steady glow
From lamps of prudent virgins in the past,

Clare's inner splendor shines within these walls.
She was the first to know these nameless joys,
To know there is no other blessedness;
To breathe a peace unknown to cluttered earth,
A Silence that is singing eloquence.

San Damiano is the taper set
Upon the lampstand of the centuries,
That from this solitude its warmth may shine
And shed its light to all within the house.

Here is the treasured pearl above price,
The tiny seed sown in the womb of earth,
The fruitful seed, alive and giving birth
To that which is become a mighty tree.

Sister Eileen Lillis

. . .

SAN DAMIANO

Polished stone,
Step by step, worn by wordless dedication
Some pain and joyful tears.
Down through the chaos of the years.
Stone upon sacred stone the slow rebuilding,
Now mossed and flower hung.
At peace in Damiano,

Dusting our dreams away,
We polish the present time,
Line upon line,
Rewriting our tales not for the telling,
But for sweet sanctification,
And a deeper peace
At San Damiano.

Soft in the cloister, sistered by the Sun,
A small bird gathers for her young,
Safely nested in the eaves.
While pimpernel, scarlet and blushing,
The poor man's weather vane,
Opens for the Sun
This is the resting place,
The harvesting of moments long waiting to be blessed;

So now with pilgrim feet,
We add our burnish to the way;
Reconciled to all our yesterdays,
And sweetly present to the heart of this today,
At San Damiano.

Rita Hills

. . .

Spouse and Handmaid of the King

Spouse and handmaid of the King,
Praises to your Savior sing.
In the mirror of his Word
Contemplate your gracious Lord.

See his birth in stable bare,
Cradled by the Virgin fair,
See his labors here below,
Tried and tempted by the foe.
See his love upon the Cross,
Dying to redeem our loss.

Now with gladness deck your soul
By his love made free and whole.
Don the garb of purity
With fair flowers of charity.

Run unstumbling in the way
Leading to the perfect day.

Praise we now our God above
He whose love inflames our love,
Whose remembrance gives sweet light
And whose graciousness delight.

May our lives reflect his grace
Till in heaven we see his face.

Susan Elisabeth

Prayer to Saint Clare

Clare, our sister and friend,
stir our fractured, fearful hearts
to embrace God's extravagant,
healing love.

Woman graced with wisdom and courage,
teach us to discern and create
opportunities for cooperation, challenge
and compassion.

Clare, our companion and guide,
inspire our choices
to be healers and reconcilers,
trusted friends of God—
reverencing all creation,
respecting each other.

Sister Joyce Harris

To Agnes (1235)

With apologies to Saint Clare
the Lord bestows the heavenly realm
on her who leaves the parents' home
of moth consumed security
for whoever links her heart
to driftwood in the river's flow
misses love
to hitch God to the race for wealth
is more than human skill can do
who lives it up in life on earth
can hardly share the reign of Christ
wise is the businessman who swoops the share scripts
in his safety box
for orphans' and widows' thankful prayers
his banknotes for the hundredfold
of loving unconditionally

Bonaventure Hinwood

FOR REFLECTION

Reflect on similarities and differences between the calls of Clare and Francis and your own call.

SUGGESTED SCRIPTURE

Ruth 1:14–18

1 Kings 17:8–24

Luke 1:26–56

NOTES

[1] "Legend of St. Clare," in *Clare of Assisi: Early Documents*, Regis J. Armstrong, ed. (St. Bonaventure, N.Y.: Franciscan Institute Publications, 1993), p. 259. Hereafter this book will be referred to as *CA:ED*, followed by page numbers. Clare would normally have accompanied the other young ladies as they went to receive their palms. It is regarded as a mark of the bishop's approval for Clare's decision to leave home that he personally came to her with a palm.

[2] Fortini, pp. 346–348.

[3] "Legend of St. Clare," *CA:ED*, p. 279.

[4] "Legend of St. Clare," *CA:ED*, p. 280.

STATION NINE: THE PORTIUNCULA

THIS LITTLE CHAPEL HAS A VERY SPECIAL PLACE IN THE HEART OF ALL Franciscans. Clare was tonsured here. Francis returned to this place to die. This station celebrates the flowering of Francis' call into the Franciscan mission and charism.

The Portiuncula is one of the three named churches that Francis restored. He was anxious to rebuild this church because it was dedicated to Our Lady of the Angels and he always had a great devotion to the Blessed Mother.

Today, like an embryo within its womb, the Portiuncula is encased inside the Basilica of St. Mary of the Angels. The tiny, dark chapel barely holds a group of thirty pilgrims. The basilica is huge, light and airy, decorated in marble.

The Portiuncula is linked with the development of all aspects of the Franciscan charism: The Franciscan Mission was the base to which brothers returned from their missionary activities for chapters. These were the opportunities to share their experiences and review their way of life. They considered which aspects of their life had to be addressed in the light of experience. Francis addressed them with words of admonition and encouragement. The brothers would also endure correction for serious lapses.

As the Order grew, chapters established administrative structures, such as provinces. From the earliest days, the friars faced contempt and persecution. When they traveled into northern Europe their orthodoxy was challenged because they had no official stamp of authorization. In some places they could not speak the local dialect and were confused with heretics. Over time a probationary period was introduced and more attention was given to formation.

Francis redefined what it was to pray with great love because of his devotion to Our Lady. He chose the brothers who would remain at the Portiuncula with particular care.[1] They were expected to be models of the life, "truly devoted to God and perfect in every respect."

The brothers lived in tiny, simple huts around the church. Francis was reluctant to see any permanent building here. He started to tear down a building, provided by the people of Assisi to accommodate the thousands of brothers during a chapter.[2] He was only stopped because the local people told him it was not his to destroy. They owned it.

Initially all the brothers gathered here for chapters. Here they were free to enjoy the spirit of Franciscan fraternity. It was their home. Together they worked out how they should live, how practical issues, like climate, would be taken into account as the missionary regions expanded.

Positioned in the plain, some brothers went out from here to offer service to local people in need. At the chapters they agreed where and how each brother should serve the kingdom. Their spirit of minority was renewed and strengthened by coming together.

This is where their penitential life was reviewed and developed. It also gave the people of Assisi an opportunity to provide for the brothers' needs, as the numbers attending increased and everyone had to be fed and given somewhere to rest.

The major decisions in Francis' life were made at the chapters, such as going to the Holy Land and resigning from the administration of the order so as to spend more time in prayer, while continuing to provide spiritual leadership through writings.

CONTRIBUTIONS

PRAISES OF GOD

You, Lord, are greater than our conscience, our problems.

You do wonders! You alone are our salvation. You are affirmation and certainty.

You, Holy Father/Mother, are our rest!

You are life's SPARKLE!

You are three and one, You are community/fraternity...

You are forgiveness; You are healer; You are conversion; You are metanoia.

Lord, God, living and faithful, You are our past, present and future.

You are Eucharist; You are food for the journey. You are contemplation, joy, love, our dwelling place.

You are our values; You, Lord, are our poverty, our vow of love, of obedience.

You are enough for me (us),

for you are resurrection and life eternal;

Father, Son and Holy Spirit! Amen! I rejoice!

Martha Delgado

. . .

PRAYER FOR FRANCISCAN UNITY

"That all may be one..." (John 17:22)

O gracious and loving Creator, having brought us into the body of Christ and called us to follow Francis and Clare: Let your Holy Spirit inspire all in the Franciscan family to be of one heart and mind in love with you and one another.

Grant, we pray, that our common
charism and vocation shared by
Franciscan orders from
Every Christian tradition help
build up the Body of Christ and
heal the Franciscan Family,
through Jesus Christ our Lord.
Amen.

Joint Committee on Franciscan Unity

. . .

SAINT FRANCIS

Seculars, Orders of Friar Minors, Conventuals, Capuchins, Third
Order Regulars
All following in Francis's footsteps
Inspired by the Holy Spirit building God's Kingdom on earth
Not losing sight of personal holiness
Transformed through metanoia, becoming lights of the world.

Francis and companions showing the way
Reaching out to the Wolf of Gubbio
Always present to the leper, to those in need
Never leaving the umbrella of the Church
Contemplation the Center of his being
Invoking God's guidance
Stigmata his blessing.

Anne Twitchell

DANCING FRANCIS

Dancing Francis
You skip
So lightly
Not touching
Not grasping
Reaching
Embracing
Something
We mortals
Do not see—
'Tis love
In guise
Lady poverty
Dare we grasp her hem
Free to
Love

Sister Mary Mansk

. . .

SUNSET

Is life so precious as years come and go? Francis, my friend, how much did you know of the loneliness and fear of each aging year, when strength for the mission may well disappear?

Did you find joy in every valley and hill, then forget to acknowledge that special thrill when our plans for tomorrow meet ache and pain, though we smile and declare it spiritual gain?

When we know we can't travel this wonderful world missing more magic of new flags unfurled, we hope our memories stay as clear as they seem and those glorious years more than a dream.

Dear Francis, you inspired us to build a church, so we know we are not rocking here in the lurch, 'twas God's love and God's joy that seasoned our lives, your belief in his power evermore survives.

Oh, how we miss working all day long, soaking up God's love like a beautiful song. But now, here we star in a brand new part. Isn't it the same with the Lord in our heart?

Edna Logsdon

. . .

PEACE

The hand of Saint Francis and the paw of the wolf, one within the other, are symbols of two opposite factions that can come together peaceably.

According to the legend, the wolf agreed to stop ravaging the town of Gubbio, and the people agreed to feed the wolf daily until its death. Mutual respect and willingness for compromise can lead to peace between individuals, among local and national groups, and among nations, even to a global level.

Mary Esther Stewart

MISSIONARY

It was so quiet, you could hear the small light flicker.
Why was it there?
There wasn't much else in the room as far as one could see
which wasn't very far.
The tiny flame had little radiance outside its glass enclosure
What was it good for?
Was it really dancing as it consumed itself to no purpose?
You may call it "fire" but, what a waste of potential!
Would there be any profit from its existence?
How would society benefit?
It was all wrapped up in its own little world,
escaping from reality,
doomed to a dreary nonexistence,
never able to assert itself.
What was its quality of life after all?
Who would remember such a small light?
And look! As it burns, it only grows smaller still!
One would point and call another
until the several watched the useless flame
consuming itself in seeming self-destruction.
Still, they marveled at its bold persistence,
its gentle perseverance,
undaunted and undimmed beneath their laughing gaze.
And then, they turned away.
Yet, that sliver of light pierced the heart
of their productive day.
Insignificant as it seemed
they could not stay away
returning to that less than beacon light

to watch it burn away
until the day the word was spread:
"The flame is nearly gone!"
So it was a crowd that gathered beneath
the last breath of fire;
but before it entirely expired,
a brown-robed poor man came through a door
no one had really noticed before.
Reverently, he genuflected in front of
what seemed to be an elevated box.
Had it always been there?
With a long taper, the gentle man rescued
the sputtering bit of flame
giving it new life atop a wax-filled globe.
Hero that he was, he did but smile
as the waiting throng heaved a deep sigh of relief.
The useless flame burned on as the busy professionals followed the
poor man through the open door to learn more about the tiny flame
and the mysterious Box.
Dancing in its glass enclosure
the sliver of light began its journey
toward smallness
as it burned
for God.

Immaculate Heart Monastery

For Reflection

1. In what ways are you inspired by Francis, Clare and the early Franciscan movement in your particular vocation?

2. Reflect on how the Franciscan charism has evolved, from your own experience.

Suggested Scripture

Matthew 5:1–16

John 6:60–71

NOTES

[1] *FA:ED II*, "The Remembrance of the Desire of a Soul," pp. 256–258.
[2] *FA:ED II*, "The Remembrance of the Desire of a Soul," pp. 285–286.

Station Ten: San Damiano

San Damiano was the home of Clare and her sisters, the Poor Ladies of San Damiano, from 1212 until after Clare's death in 1253. She was canonized in 1255. The process of canonization has left us a record of important details of the manner of her life, including miracles.

For most of its history San Damiano has belonged to the Order of Friars Minor. After her death, St. Clare's Basilica was built in Assisi, on the site of the parish church of San Giorgio, to honor Saint Clare and for the safekeeping of her relics. Pope Alexander IV commissioned a proto-monastery for the Poor Ladies, which was completed in 1260. The community brought the San Damiano crucifix with them. It now hangs in a side chapel where it is still venerated today.

Clare's way of life changed as she grew closer to God. For a time, Clare lived an extremely ascetical life, eating almost nothing, sleeping on bare stone, wearing a hair shirt. Over time, on the advice of Francis and Bishop Guido, she relaxed her fast a little. Later she warned against the dangers of excessive fasting. She started to accept straw bedding and removed her hair shirt. Having initially resisted, she agreed to accept the title of abbess, because it was better for the community to observe the usual practice of having an abbess.

Clare steadfastly insisted on two principles:

1. The community at San Damiano was to preserve absolute poverty. Gregory IX sought to absolve the community from total poverty but Clare refused to be absolved from following the poverty of Christ. She devoted much of her life to fighting for the privilege of poverty. She refused any financial security. Alms were provided, often

brought by Franciscan brothers. The sisters kept enough land to grow crops for subsistence, but not for profit or to have excess. Sisters were all expected to undertake manual work, such as spinning. Clare herself made several cloths, often for use in churches.

2. Franciscan brothers would continue to provide a spiritual service for the Poor Ladies. Clare threatened that the community would go on hunger strike if, as Pope Gregory IX recommended in 1230, the brothers were replaced by other priests as chaplains. She stated that if the sisters were to be deprived of their spiritual food, they would refuse to eat.

San Damiano was designed for a life of enclosure, yet Clare was well-informed about developments within the church and the first order.

There were many visitors who brought news and, in turn, spread reports of how the Poor Ladies lived. Among these were some of Francis' closest companions, but changes in the Order of Friars Minor resulted in most brothers having less time and commitment to serve the sisters. The friars were often settled within urban areas, carrying out pastoral duties, in fixed communities and financially secure. The church remained anxious that monasteries of women should have a certain security.

Clare decided to compose a rule for her sisters to safeguard the way of life that had evolved in the community. She was the first woman to write a rule for a religious community. It was based on existing monastic rules, the *Later Rule* of the O.F.M., and community life experience. Clare's *Form of Life* provides insights into the spirit by which the sisters lived.

Primary emphasis was placed on following the gospel. Although enclosed, it was possible for sisters to leave the monastery for approved purposes. Within the community, sisters were to be very solicitous in their relations, putting the needs of others before their own. Silence was not as rigidly imposed as in other enclosed communities. Weekly chapters allowed all the sisters to have a voice.

There were certain sisters who served outside the monastery and maintained contact between the city and the monastery. These women dealt with any business affairs. It is clear, from the process of canonization, that many witnesses were impressed by Clare's loving care for her sisters, especially the weak and infirm. She continued manual work throughout her prolonged illness. Clare encouraged her sisters to be mirrors or exemplars to everyone.

Four of Clare's letters to Agnes of Prague have survived. From these we learn something of how Clare contemplated the Lord before the crucifix. Like Francis, she was inspired by the depth of God's love, wonderfully expressed in the humility and poverty of Jesus.

Clare keenly felt the loss of Francis when he died in 1226. About three years later she lost her sisters from the San Damiano community, when she was asked to become abbess at Monticello in Florence.

Clare is called Francis' little plant because she transplanted Franciscan ideals of prayer, poverty, humility and sorority within the very different environment of a fixed cloister. She burned with great love and desire for Christ. She devoted herself to discerning and following the Father's will.

CONTRIBUTIONS

POOR CLARE

Taking the plain brown stuff of each new day
you stretch it taut upon a steel-strong frame
wrought from silence. With prayer as thread
you stitch a cross for every moment given,
until no space on this firm fabric is unfilled.
Love forms your needle, bright and skilled
from constant touch, piercing to bind
warp and weft in steadfast unity.
When your colors blend and harmonize—
earth tones of misted hill and tree,
flowing river, rock and weathered skies—
they become sweet music, silver
symphony shot with gold and laced
with flame for quiet suffering.
And what you have in centered patience traced
is a rich gift, and precious, for a King.
We would give you, who watch, the key
to unlock the riddle of this tapestry.

Michaela Davis

. . .

PRAYER TO SAINT CLARE

O blessed Lady Clare, we come before you as daughters and sons of
Saint Francis and beg your healing intercession on behalf of our sisters and associates [family, friends and those closest to us] who are

ill. Just as you signed your sisters with the sign of the cross, healing them in the dormitory of San Damiano, so we too sign ourselves now in prayer. May this simple gesture remind us that if our gaze is fixed on Jesus, we will be transformed and healed in His redeeming love. May all of our sisters and associates who we are lifting in prayer and who are ill know of God's profound love for them. May they be at peace knowing that we are deeply grateful for the graces their suffering bestows on our congregation [us all]. We ask all this in God's name, Amen.

Joanne Schatzlein

. . .

COME, CLARE, SHARE WITH US YOUR VISION

Come, Clare, share with us your vision
Beneath and beyond what earthly eyes discern
As God's only Son, in deep humility,
Came from the brilliance of Uncreated Word,
To draw our hearts to gaze with awe and rapture,
At Triune Beauty, hid in human form.
Made to agonize for love's refusal,
To be a step below Almighty Power.
With gentle Innocence he came amongst us,
His Father's image to restore again,
His hidden life, His Cross, His Death, and Rising,
Destined to manifest the Heart of God.
While mirrored in the human face of Jesus,
God's love reflecting on our souls once more,
May we become that love's reflection daily,
That by Eternal Glory we may be,

Beloved of the Eternal Father,
One with Him, in whom He is well pleased.

Sister Collette McDonnell

. . .

CANTICLE OF CLARE

My soul rejoices in God's compassionate love
for He never forgets or ignores the lowly. By His greatness the suffer-
    ing and pain in my lowly flesh
have become joyful penance
for He carries the cross with me. The lowly one's self-renunciation in
    embracing my own poverty
becomes an exquisite pleasure to the Poor Christ
for He happily shares His poverty of humanity with me.
He fills the thirsting soul with the fullness of spirit of love, saying,
    "You are most chaste for you have loved me faithfully with your
    whole being."
As the lowly flesh longs for Him in contemplation,
He stoops down and touches me with tender lips, whispering in my
    ear, "You are made pure by my kiss for I am pouring out a new
    spirit within you."
As the unworthy one accepts His loving kiss with a whole heart, He
    gently embraces me with sweet whispers of love, "Your pure and
    humble heart has made you virgin, so, from now on, you are a vir-
    gin forever whom I joyfully contemplate."
There is nothing more precious than to possess the virtues of the
    Lord: His poverty, humility and charity.
Whose poverty that bears the spiritual joy teaches me to be my true
    self in giving up the possession of a false self.

Whose charity the poor in spirit desires brings the heavenly kingdom
with the promise of a new life. Whose compassion the sinners
and the lowly ones hope for
bestows the fullness of life and forgiveness to lead them to the everlasting.
Whose generosity that does not distinguish from age, color, nation,
culture, and class.
gives His pleasant fragrance to all those who desire Him.
Whose humility that manifests in His Incarnation invites the lowly
and poor
into the marvelous joy and pleasure.
Whose beauty all the natures and pure-hearted souls
unceasingly sing with great admiration.
Holy is His name and Mercy is His desire for the poor and lowly.
Therefore, my daughters;
Come, the poor in spirit and the lowly ones, to possess the richness
of God's goodness and power.
Come, those who endure the hardship and pain, to rejoice in the
happiness of the new life in the resurrection of the Lord.
Come, those who carry heavy burdens and weaknesses,
to the Sacred Heart where the perfect Holy One invites and embraces
you with ineffable affection.
Come, the pure and humble of virgins,
to sing the delightful praises to the Most High and Glorious God.
Come, God's loved ones
He cares for your inmost hearts that He created in you for He desires
to dwell in you.
Come, those who have tasted God's goodness,
come with your whole heart, then you will be filled with all the
graces of joy and peace, and with the sweetest fragrance of Him.

My beloved daughters,
always rejoice in God in giving yourself to Him totally
for He has loved you with an everlasting love
and He is constant in His affection for you, in your lowliness.

Rita Cheong

. . .

LITANY OF SAINT CLARE

Response: Saint Clare pray for us.

After conversion, the Lord gave you sisters—give us love in the charity of Christ—let us grow in the love of God—through building San Damiano, your ladies glorified God and church—having entered the Way of God, let us not turn back on the Lord, his Mother, and dear brother Francis—keep us aware of pride, vainglory, envy, distractions of the world—help us preserve unity and love.

The bond of perfection—remind us to thank God for our vocation—make our needs known in love according to the Spirit—little Mother of your sisters, help us to be approachable in the needs of our sisters—through the Gospel let us follow Jesus, his Mother, Francis and persevere until the end—help us to know the Son of God to come lead us on the Way—as pilgrims assist us in the footsteps of Jesus—help us support others interested in following Jesus—remind us to bless and praise God at all times—remind us to thank God for all creation—remind us to pray for all missionaries—intercede to God to enlighten our hearts by His mercy and grace to do penance—help us to place our minds before the mirror of eternity, our soul in the brightness of glory, our hearts in the figure of divine substance and our whole selves through contemplation in the image of God.

Praise and bless the Lord and give Him thanks to be able to serve Him. Amen.

Sister Ramona Kruse

.   .   .

O BLESSED CLARE

O Blessed Clare,
you were a light in your day,
radiating the joy and peace
   of knowing Jesus.
Be a light to us on our
journey. Gently lead us
to that deep and lasting
union with our Divine Lover.
Help us to put our complete
trust in the One who loves us,
so that we, too, may pour out
our lives in service.
Gracious Clare, teach us
your way of openness and
gratitude to every gift of God.

Sister Barbara Borst

RECONCILIATION OF OPPOSITES

Clara was from a noble landed family. She prayed and did works of charity from her home before joining Francis. She was a pious young lady.

Francis was the son of a merchant whose wealth was in coins and money, not in land. He was a dissolute young man dressing and partying lavishly.

Both left the city but Francis was a mover and he got to Egypt and the Holy Land in the East and Spain in the West. He went out to towns and cities as well as hermitages to seek the outcasts. Once Clara was settled in San Damiano, she never left, but the lowly as well as the high and mighty were welcomed to visit her but were not to enter the Cloister.

Clara longed to have Francis and the Friars visit. She welcomed these visits as she depended on their spiritual and material help.

Francis avoided visits to Clara and allowed a prohibition in his final rule that forbade visits of Friars to the monastery of nuns. They needed permission from the Holy See, to visit nuns.

Letters were written by Francis to rulers, friars, all of the faithful, the brothers and sisters of penance but none to Clara.

Clara wrote her own rule, the first woman to do so, she wrote letters to Agnes of Prague but we have no letters to Francis.

Clara lived, though she suffered from a long illness, until she was sixty.

Francis died after many illnesses in his mid-forties.

Francis wanted nothing to do with coins or money. His Friars were not even to touch them. The Friars were also to own no houses or places or anything. Clara's privilege of poverty was not to own income-producing property.

Clara was certainly influenced by Francis but she was her own woman who influenced Francis and the friars as well as church leaders and others. These two both followed the gospel though in many different ways.

This difference of our Father and Mother lets us know that their Spiritual children can be, and are, very different witnesses. Bonaventure, Juniper, Joseph of Cupertino, John of Capestrano, Angela of Foligno, Colette, Margaret of Cortona all have very different character yet embraced Christ and his Gospel by following them, creatively moved by the Spirit.

Juniper Cummings, O.F.M., CONV.

. . .

ON THE CROSS I SEE

During March and June 1225, Francis stayed at San Damiano for fifty or more days. Less well known is the discourse with Clare that occurred the day after. From the sources we learn that she and the sisters were greatly worried about his health. Francis wanted to visit to consult and comfort them. The result was this short dialogue with Clare, the other Sisters, and Brother Leo who accompanied him to San Damiano. (Francis still had the cautery mark on his face and he could not endure the light of day.)

Clare: Father, why do you refuse the cure? Would it not be proper to go? And, if the medicine is appropriate, why is there more infection? You are not resting and we rest with the sun. Who is taking care of this poor one?

Francis: It is He whom is coming and He who continues to call. Do you not hear?

Clare: I don't understand your words, why do you say, "who comes"? Who is coming and who is continuing to call?

117

Francis: He alone, who you want to see coming. Do you not hear how pleasing is His voice? Don't you see also with the eyes of the heart, the beauty which comes dancing through the hills?

Clare: How can I hear, that which is already given you to see? Where is the voice which you say "comes"?

Francis: Do you not feel how it is pleasing? Do you not listen also to the warm breeze which comes down the valley and the birds singing in the distance....Do you not hear the words spoken to you? And you, loving sisters, do you not hear how it is sweet, since it is He who speaks?

Clare: Father, how it is ruinous being where you already are, and seeing what you see. But consider us still, avoiding leaving us in sorrow.

Francis: Don't fear. He already lives and is present in the heart, which is tormented and has the love which it is not possible to see. Don't you feel that sweet words continue to whisper? Do you not hear also His pleasant voice which says, "Rise my friend, my beauty and come!" Here the winter is past, and ceasing to rain, now the flowers are appearing in the fields. The time for the song has begun and the voice of the dove is now heard anew in our land.

Clare: They who desire, all who will to hear, can have this consolation of the cross.

Francis: They, if hearing, don't have fear. If you see all the splendor of Him, this will give you the peace for which you are looking, because the beauty of Him staggers in love. His word clears every sorrow. His love cleans the rusty armor in which the soul suffers for the lack of proper and true purity.

Clare: Where is it possible to see this, faithful Father? Leave to search, we want to see. The talk, also for our good, is disturbing us, while we are hearing you speak to us, who also contemplates his indescribable splendor.

Francis: Clare, don't you see Him who is present? Don't you feel the one who continues to call you, the one burning with love for Him?

Clare: Where, holiest Father? Where is the voice of Him? Where is His face to be seen? Don't keep us in suspense with these words of yours.

Francis: The cross is that which is present, and that which issues forth splendor. It is this beauty which many have ravished, because from it proceeds words of love, which only the loving heart can hear. Don't you listen to what it says? Don't you look at Him who calls, offering His love with arms extended for you to hold?

Clare: Enkindle in my heart light words. I sing my song to the King. My song, my tongue is like a pen of a scribe. You are the fairest of the Sons of Man. From the lips is diffused grace. You are Blessed by God forever.

Francis: Now you comprehend what I wanted to say. Not wanting to frighten you, I feared coming. That love of His which now you sing of is His ineffable beauty. He awaits to finally drink again in the celestial life. What was, is always the sorrow of the one who so suffers. What was the impression of suffering before this vision of consolation, that which surpasses every good. If this is the gift with which you are recompensed for your fatigue, what is there possibly yet to discover? Also not wanting you to go, while not hearing the voice but following the decisions of the voice of he who continues to call?

Clare: I go without wavering and every impression is pleasing and light to support.

Francis: This is the priority to which you should attend. There is nothing to make up again in view of so much love. The love outside is nothing compared to the pleasure of the union with Him who is life and breath. Neither is there any greater good for you and the sisters who have left all for following his footsteps and his words. For the life which is lived with much suffering, also for you, where there is much suffering and privation, all this is nothing in comparison to the joy which follows the experience of your love. The cross is your good.

Clare: There's no other one to look for, we say, where is it possible to see and contemplate the beauty of our delight which now inflames so many? He comes dancing on the hills, and He calls with the voice so fair in the profundity of heart saying these words, which everyone wants to hear, "O my dove, who is in the crevice of the rock, do not hide from my grasp, grant me your sight. Let me hear your voice, because your voice is pleasant, your sight is elegant."

Francis: Go then meet without delay. Don't abandon the invitation. Give to Him your time, and to the others concealed with you. He is not a long way off, hidden from you calling on His name. But He is in the vicinity. And He is Father, and the Love of which you have need. He will remain, even if I don't see you again, and take leave of my body, at length certainly worn out. But to Him who conducts His love, love Him only, because He is One, Good, Yours and Mine. And He is the Lord Whom we love!

Anthony Sejda

FOR REFLECTION

What aspects of Clare's life inspire you the most?

SUGGESTED SCRIPTURE

Psalm 103

The Song of Solomon, 2:8–17

Luke 1:46–56

THE LITTLE TOWN OF GRECCIO IS LOCATED ON A RIDGE OF A MOUNTAIN THAT overlooks the Rieti Valley. It is located on the route that Francis took when traveling between Rome and Assisi. John Velita, a local man, gave Francis and the brothers a site on the mountainside close by. This became another hermitage for the brothers. Inside it seems just like an extension of the mountainside.

This is where Francis recreated a living Nativity scene. The chapel resembles a cave. There is a fresco with two pictures of the infant Jesus. Francis is depicted kneeling at the manger, in front of the baby Jesus, wrapped in swaddling clothes. Next to this, Jesus, dressed exactly the same way, is being fed from his mother's breast, mother and child lovingly gazing at each other. These frescoes convey love, trust, reverence and peace. They express the absolute dependency of the baby Jesus on his mother.

Today there is a new church outside the hermitage area that contains a large tableau representing all the details of the Nativity narratives from the Gospels of Luke and Matthew, including the Massacre of the Innocents and the Flight to Egypt.

Francis first visited Greccio in 1217 when his preaching drew many of the local people to repentance. In 1223 he asked John Velita to prepare a Christmas celebration to which everyone was invited. His desire was to replicate the scene of the first Christmas at the midnight Mass. An empty manger was placed at the center of the scene, to remind people of the simplicity, poverty and humility of his Lord on the occasion of his birth.

Francis, dressed as a deacon, preached on the theme of the poverty of Christ at the Incarnation. During the Mass, Celano records that a man saw "a beautiful little child asleep in that manger and saw the holy man of God approach the child and waken him from a deep sleep." Bonaventure embellishes the story with a description of Francis embracing the infant in his arms.[1] The scene is full of the tenderness and love Francis felt for the little child.

Clare was inspired by the poverty of Jesus, wrapped in swaddling clothes and lying in a manger. One Christmas, she was too ill to attend Mass with her sisters, which caused her great sadness. Suddenly, she was able to hear the brothers singing from the Basilica of St. Francis. It was as if she were physically present.[2] She also saw the manger of baby Jesus. On another occasion, when receiving the Eucharist, she saw the Lord's body, like a very small and beautiful young boy.[3]

Francis and Clare experienced the greatness of God's love in their lives. They discovered new ways to contemplate divine love, expressed most fully for them in the Incarnation, on the Cross and in the Eucharist. This helped them to know the Lord intimately and inflamed their desire to serve him more and more faithfully, and follow him more closely. Both had a deep devotion to Our Lady.

CONTRIBUTIONS

THEN AND...NOW BETHLEHEM...GRECCIO...TODAY'S WORLD

Unbridled hunger for wealth and political power prevailed...

A clashing dichotomy between the rich and the poor existed...Constant wars punctuated the times...

The marginalized suffered from neglect...

Francis, how much you must have been pained to see in your day how God had been forgotten! The stirring of the Spirit moved your soul and you responded. You made real at Greccio the Gift of Incarnation! Passionately, you wanted to remind the inhabitants of your world how much God loved them.

So, on Christmas Eve, 1223, Greccio became Bethlehem all over again—with a *real* creche, a *real* ox and ass, and *real* shepherds. You brought Jesus to life again!

O Jesus, how much You must love us that You entered into our human condition!

We thank and praise You, Almighty God, for what You have accomplished through Your Servant, Francis. Help us, whom You have called to walk in the footsteps of Francis, to make the Incarnation come alive in today's world, again. We ask this through Jesus, Your Son. Amen.

Sister Mary Bandurski

. . .

CLARE'S LAST CHRISTMAS

In the dormitory darkness, an icy wind
gnawed at the rafters above her. The straw mat
jabbed at her right shoulder. She thought of Jesus,
the Baby-God spending his first night
on a bed of straw, and offered her pain.
Each of her sisters had begged to stay,
but Clare, knowing Midnight Mass with the brothers
with San Francesco would give them strength
for the dark path ahead of them, had insisted,
"I will sleep. I want you all to go."

A nearby rustle startled her wide awake.
How many more mice were feasting downstairs
on the cheeses and bread which the brothers
had brought? She chided herself for worrying.
Weren't the mice God's creatures, too?

The darkness grew more menacing.
If only she could see the stars!
A faint light glowed from the bottom
of the stairs. She blessed the sister
who had left a candle burning there.
In her dream, she was eighteen again.
The Palm Sunday moon, nearly full, revealed
where the key was hidden. She unlocked
the garden gate and crept down Assisi's cobblestoned
streets. Dogs snuffled, then quietly licked her hands.
She slipped through the city gate into the Valley
of Spoleto. The moon peered through olive trees
and drew monstrous shadows on the narrow path.
An owl screeched. She heard a sudden cry of terror
in the underbrush ahead. Then all was still again.
Shouldn't she have reached the Portiuncula
by now? Had she taken the wrong path?
She forced herself to a steady pace, taking
one step, another, one step, another.
Beyond this night, she knew, there would be
no path at all. She herself would have to make it.
She stopped. No, she would not go back!
It was God who called her forward.

And then she heard the Brothers singing
as they came to meet her with lighted candles.
She heard the Christmas chant: *Dominus dixit*
ad me! but knew she was no longer dreaming.
She watched her sisters gather at the crèche near the altar
as a brother laid the baby in a manger so near
that she could almost hear the infant breathing.

Irene Zimmerman, O.S.F.

· · ·

Some Thoughts on Saint Francis and the Birth of Jesus

Jesus had been dead or asleep in many hearts, but Francis had been His voice and His example and again restored the Divine Child to life and awakened it from its trance.

The spiritual life of Saint Francis, his devotional life, is sometimes abbreviated in the formula "The Crib, the Cross and the Altar." From all eternity, Christ exists in the mind of God as King, the Priest and the Prophet of the universe. Because of Adam's sin, Jesus also had to take on the role of the Redeemer of mankind. The act of our redemption began when the Word became flesh, when Mary said "yes," when the Word of God entered a tiny cell in her womb.

For nine months, Jesus was His mother's "private property." Her very body, as Saint Francis said, was "His Palace, His Tabernacle, His Robe." Then in a cave that sheltered animals, He was brought forth and given to the whole world.

For the next thirty-three years He prepared Himself and us for His sacrificial death on the Cross. As proof that this sacrifice was accepted by God the Father, He was gloriously restored to life at the Resurrection. And at every Mass, in the finest cathedral or in the poorest of chapels, whether he be a wise theologian or a very simple priest, a great saint or a great sinner, at *every* Mass, Jesus looked after all Saint Francis' wishes very faithfully. During the Mass, he had a vision during which it seemed to him that he saw a real child lying in the manger, but as if dead or sleeping. Then Brother Francis stepped forward and took it lovingly in his arms. The child smiled at Francis and with its little hands stroked his bearded chin and his coarse habit. But this vision did not surprise John in the least. For Jesus had been dead or asleep in many hearts, but Francis had been His voice and His example and again restored the Divine Child to life and awakened it from its trance.

Christ is born again and Calvary is renewed, repeated, perpetuated on our altars. As God looks down on those altars, He does not hear the splendid harmony of a well-trained choir or the discordant sounds of a poorly trained choir, He does not smell the incense in the censer nor the sweat of unwashed bodies, He pays no attention at all to the fine garments or the tattered rags of the congregation. He sees only His beloved Son and the mystical continuation of the Sacrifice that bought our redemption.

In the mind of Saint Francis, these three things, the crib, the cross and the altar, were so closely intertwined that he could not think of any one of them without considering the other two as well.

Lee Lampe

DEAR MARY

Dear Mary,
Can I hold your Baby Jesus
just for a little while?
Can I look upon His face
and hope that He will smile?
Can I hold your Baby Jesus
and feel the love you share?
Will I hand Him back to you
the pain too much to bear?
Do I have a mother's love for Him
and want to keep him near?
Or do I turn my back
hiding in my fear?
Does someone else take care of Him
when I turn away?
Or does he cry for me,
asking me to stay?

Can I hold your Baby Jesus
When they take Him from the Cross?
Can I stand here right beside you
and feel a mother's loss?
I love your Baby Jesus!
Let me hold Him for awhile.
I will keep Him safe for you
while He is still a child.
Be still, my Baby Jesus.
I do love you so. Your mother let me hold You,
'Cause she wanted you to know.

Kate Kleinart

Be Praised O My God

Be praised O my God, for my mother's life
which you have made fragrant
with the perfume of the Holy Spirit
and with prayer;
which you created at her conception
and ransomed at her second conception
in the saving waters of baptism.

Be praised for leading her
into a gentleness
which you say will inherit the earth
and which makes her resemble you
who are gentle.
Be praised for giving her strength
in suffering evil and injustice
without bitterness
for you
who are mercy and forgiveness.

Be praised O my God,
for giving her fire in her heart—
which though it may burn
also purifies and heals,
like you, who are a burning fire.

Be praised for all the goodness you have given her,
for of herself
she is nothing
and all her goods come from you.

Be praised for giving her Life:
Life worth struggling for,
Life worth suffering for,
Life worth dying for,
you who are Life.

Be praised O my God, for my mother's life
and for all the love you have given me
through her and for her. Amen.

Loarne Ferguson

.   .   .

In Praise of Our God

You are Alpha, all in all, attentive, amazing, abundance
You are Bridegroom, being, beauty, breath of life
You are Creator, complete, caring, companion, courage, clarity
You are Divinity, dear, dynamic, dawn and dusk
You are Ever-ancient and ever-new, evergreen, everlasting
You are Father, friend, fullness of life, freedom, future
You are Gift, generous, gentle, good, giving
You are Holy, hope for the hopeless, home, help for all
You are Infinity, inspiring, immeasurable, illuminating
You are Justice, jewel, journey
You are King, kindness, knowing
You are Light, loving, life-giving, luminous
You are Maker, my God, Mother, mystery, most high,
You are Now, near, ever-near
You are Omega, omnipotent, overwhelming, orderly
You are Peace, presence, playful, praiseworthy

You are Quiet, questioning
You are Rock, revered, refreshment
You are Sacred, Spouse, security, strength, song-spiriting
You are Truth, tranquility, transformation
You are Universal, understanding, unconditional love
You are Victorious, vision, voice for the voiceless
You are Wisdom, wholeness, wonder, wine of life
You are Xerox, (e)xample for all the saints
You are Yahweh, You are You
You are Zenith of love and perfection, Zion—a dwelling place

Sister de Lellis Albert, O.S.F.

.   .   .

NIGHT PRAYER

Why do I want the moon
when there are so many stars in the sky?
I've seen the moon shining bright.
It may be only clouds that cover the moon
and keep its light from me.

But, I'm not good at living with just starlight.
Then again, maybe it will just take
the patience to wait for a new day,
so I can see, O Lord, the brightness of your love,
surrounding me, flooding the world
and making it a beautiful place to behold.

Lord, help me to know your presence
in my night times
and

in the dawn
the warmth of your love.

Mary Ryk

. . .

My Ears Have Heard the Music of the Herald of the King

My ears have heard the music of the herald of the King
as he danced the hills of Umbria God's praises glad to sing
while calling us to journey to our home in heaven above
in poverty and love.

Praise we now the King of heaven,
sing all peoples alleluia,
Christ who came to dwell among us
in the fullness of his love.

My life will speak in silence of the splendor of his grace
as I kneel in contemplation of the beauty of his face,
as I bow in supplication that the world may be set free
by the Son who died for me.

Praise and glory to the Saviour,
sing all peoples alleluia,
worship Jesus the Redeemer
who died to win our love.

My eyes have seen the radiance of the everlasting hills
and my ears have heard the music which all earthly clamor stills,
my heart is filled with longing for my Lord in heaven above
and the fullness of his love.

Glory be to God the Father,
sing all peoples alleluia,
praise to Son and Holy Spirit,
blest Trinity of Love.

Susan Elisabeth

. . .

THE GIFT

Thank you, Lord,
for what is beautiful on this earth,
especially for the birds.
As I walk through the park on a spring morning
and see them in flight and in song—
Tanangers, Orioles, Warblers, Cardinals;
Scarlet, fire orange, black—they seem so joyful, so free.
Do they sing in praise of You?
Perhaps not,
but as I watch them
my heart grows full.
And if I could sing,
it would be I who would sing songs in praise of You,
for all the beauty You have shown me.
Especially, the birds.

Christine Pratt-Scanlon

THE TALE OF THE STRAW

There was a time when I, pale, dull but useful straw,
Oft-gathered, strewn then cast away,
Did know a sweetness rare,
When special beams of starlight and heavenly light appeared,
And I did hold so humbly a tiny infant child,
And my pale and dulled drabness was changed to shining gold,
As I held so very gently the precious sleeping one,
Emmanuel, Christ Jesus had now to earth been born,
And I felt part of the Herald's light
As I basked in the heavenly rays,
Which shone in the night, the wondrous night,
Awaiting the bright new day,
Which would dawn to greet the Prince of Peace,
Who came from realms above,
Who is our daystar and our joy,
And brings God's gift of love,
This sweetness rare was mine to know,
When heaven did meet with earth below.

Ellen Spencer

. . .

CROFT MEADOWS CANTICLE, AUGUST 2005

Praise you Lord that I hear you in the gentle breeze,
The cooing of the dove,
The ripple of the water.
But it is in the silence of my own heart
That I hear your still, small voice
Speaking only to me.

Loving Lord, I thank you for the gift of touch;
Hands that brought me into this world,
Hands that tended and nurtured me,
Hands that embrace and hold me
And your pierced hands
That will reach out and lead me
And touch and enfold me
Into eternal Life.
Lord, thank you for the gift of touch.

Often I watch the rain falling from the sky;
Water from the heavens gives us life;
The thirsty earth drinks it in.
It turns my thoughts to God,
The fountain of all Life,
And my parched soul is revived.
I lift up my eyes to the hills, there I find my rest.

I thank you for your creation
For your presence in the warmth of the Son,
Filling me with your love.
Lord you are beyond wonderful,
Making such intricate cells, glands, nerve endings
And all in the right place—
Each knowing which sense is its job.

Thank you, Lord, for the sense of taste.
Thank you, Lord, for the gift of all the senses,
All of which pick up on the variety of Life,
The good, the bad and the ugly.
Praise God!
For every creature announces and proclaims,
"God made me for you, O people!"

Marion Wooliscroft

GOD'S GIFTS

A sparrow at the feeder
A woodpecker in the tree
The beauty of a sunrise
God made these things for me
The uniqueness of a snowflake
The softness of a cloud
The whisper of the wind
Sometimes soft, sometimes loud
The birth of an infant
A smile on a face
The hug of a child, a warm embrace
All made possible by God's loving grace.

Alice Kenat

. . .

FRANCIS AT HILFIELD (OCTOBER 4TH)

Brother of all things, blesséd Francis,
For you, creation, in songs and dances
Interrelated
Anticipated
Our ecological advances.
"Let all things their Creator bless!"
Those who would Jesus' name confess
Need look no higher
Than this cow-byre
To "worship Him in humbleness."
For to be human is to know

The fruits of love and joy which grow (though dust art thou
Both then and now)
From such poor humus fashioned so.
Into His image, whose loving breath
"For purpose of life," (so Francis saith)
breathed into birth
His son on earth   ·
"Love is a movement towards death."

Denis Parry

FOR REFLECTION

Contemplate the Incarnation, in the light of the understanding
that Francis and Clare had of this mystery of Christ's poverty and
humility.

SUGGESTED SCRIPTURE

Matthew 1:18–2:18
Luke 2:1–20

NOTES
[1] *FA:ED II*, "The Major Life of Saint Francis," p. 610.
[2] As a consequence, Clare was proclaimed patroness of television by Pope Pius XII in 1958.
[3] *CA:ED*, "The Acts of the Process of Canonization," p. 167.

STATION TWELVE: LA VERNA

THIS STATION IS ON A MOUNTAIN ABOUT SEVENTY MILES NORTH OF ASSISI. Francis and his brothers were given the whole mountain by Lord Orlando, Count of Chiusi in May 1213, as official records confirm.[1]

The story about how this came about appears in the First Consideration of the Holy Stigmata, part two of the *Fioretti*.[2] Francis and Leo were traveling to Romagna and happened to pass near the Castle of Montefeltro where there were great festivities because one of the counts of Montefeltro was being knighted. No doubt, Francis enjoyed the atmosphere and the troubadour singing, remembering his former dreams of knighthood. He and Leo seized the opportunity of preaching in the piazza. Francis' reputation had already grown and the people listened attentively. Orlando was personally touched by Francis' words. Francis agreed to meet with him after the feast. Orlando was so inspired that he offered the brothers a place of retreat: "A mountain in Tuscany which is very solitary and wild and perfectly suited for someone who wants to do penance in a place far from people or who wants to live a solitary life."[3]

Francis was meeting all the brothers for the Pentecost chapter at the Portiuncula. From there he agreed to dispatch two brothers to Orlando at Chiusi. They would assess the suitability of the mountain for periods of solitude and contemplation.

The brothers had difficulty finding the castle in this remote spot. When they finally arrived, the count greeted them warmly and provided them with an escort of fifty knights, to protect them from wild animals and to help set up a suitable hermitage. The brothers accepted the gift and returned to Francis where they praised and thanked God for such generosity. Francis immediately decided to spend the coming Lent in honor of Saint Michael at the hermitage.[4]

The story illustrates Francis' growing intimacy with God during this active period of his ministry.

THE IMPORTANCE OF SILENCE[5]

Francis made this retreat with Masseo, Leo and Angelo. Masseo was "mother" or guardian for the little group, meaning that he would deal with other people if the need arose, such as begging a little bread or requesting shelter. On the journey, they remained silent except when praying the office or discussing spiritual matters.

One night as they were traveling, they found a little church for shelter. Francis was attacked by demons and spent a vigil in deep prayer, endurance and patience until the devils went away. Francis went into the nearby forest to pray, and there his companions saw him weeping aloud, as if he were witnessing the Passion of Christ with his own eyes.[6]

Francis made six visits to La Verna in 1213, 1216, 1218, 1220, 1223 and 1224. During these years he became increasingly unwell, enduring multiple painful physical ailments. He also experienced the heartache of spiritual pain at some of the necessary developments in the now large Order of Friars Minor and on his last visit he received the stigmata.

Francis was willing to embrace the cross in a new way. He wanted to be part of the actual sufferings of Christ, spiritual as well as physical. He was prepared to share Christ's feeling of utter abandonment expressed in the words, "My God, my God, why have you forsaken me?" He desired complete union, sharing both Christ's total darkness and the sublime light of unconditional love. God responded.

Francis returned to his brothers. Filled with compassion, he wrote the *Praises of God* on the reverse side of the *Blessing for Brother Leo*. He lived another two years, during which his sufferings increased. In the *First Life*, Celano describes the cauterization of Francis' eyes in detail. Later, he describes his organs failing. At the same time, he describes his simplicity, humility, service, obedience, his work at reconciling enemies and the strength that others gained from being with him.

There are also hints of tensions within the order and how certain brothers grieved Francis through their lack of simplicity. He prayed for those who were not able to live as simply as he and he also realized that the order would be in God's hands, so he no longer interfered directly in the affairs of his companions.[7]

CONTRIBUTIONS

IMAGE OF THE CRUCIFIED

Crucify yourself to me:
Place your trembling hands
on my wounded palms.
Allow my Blood
to wash you
free of fear.
Crucify yourself to me:
Lay your faltering heart
against my pierced heart.
Press the Life-flow
from me to you
in crucified love.

Sister M. Anita Holzmer, O.S.F.

MOUNT ALVERNA

The flame-white stars hung trembling in the sky,
In silence keeping vigil. Earth and air,
Deep woods and living waters seemed to share
The hours of waiting, though they knew not why
They waited thus, with neither stir nor sigh,
But lay in the rapt stillness of a prayer
Before the face of God; while on the bare
Bleak mountainside he knelt in ecstasy.
And he, who read within all things the name
Of God-made-man, poured out to heaven that night
The homage of the listening stars and earth,
Till, five times pierced by love's consuming flame,
He knew divine communion; and the light
Of dawn's first glory hailed a new day's birth.

Sister Frances Ledwith, O.S.C.

. . .

STIGMATA

High on Alverno's windswept ledge
a jutting rock his pedestal.
O'er head a dark sky canopy.
He knelt and groaned, he sighed and wept,
Absorbed in God,
in love above. This little poor man, emaciated, ill clad,
irregular breaths that came with labor, to touch with numbed
    fingers, cold,
to touch his God.

A victim for man's sins.

And suddenly, in wondrous glory

there appeared in dazzling glory,

a Seraph embedded with the Crucified One!

Six wings ablaze,

two above,

two below,

two stretched outward

toward the startled figure

and in an instant shooting fiery darts,

the pain of Divine Love into this trembling body,

hands and feet and a sear-corn side. Ecstatic, Francis has Jesus'
wounds

embedded in his flesh! Wounds of pain, Wounds of blood, with
sighs and tears, in agony. Reaching out in mind and heart

wounds of the Eternal God,

A Signature of pure love! Eternal Love meeting human love,

for all to see, for all to know. Francis' eternal cry, "My Lord and My
God,

My God and My All!"

Sister M. Kevin Brand

.   .   .

STEVIE'S PRAYER

Hello Jesus My Friend,

Jesus, I would like to be able to run and play with the other kids,

But since you have other plans for me, I choose your plan today.

Jesus, for others who hurt you today by saying bad things,

Use my silent mouth to make up for the way they hurt you.

Jesus, for those who listened to things today that made you sad,
I heard a bird sing to make you glad. Jesus, for those who use their
hands or feet to hurt others,
You can use my hands and feet to be a blessing for others,
Jesus, for all families that don't love each other,
I give you my family to show them how to love.
Come Jesus, to think in my mind, to circulate in my blood,
To breathe in my breathing, to beat in my heart.
Come Jesus, you live in me and let me live in you.
Jesus, I LOVE YOU.

Stevie Busam
(Sent in by his mother, Jill. Stevie suffered from cerebral
palsy but provided amazing witness to Christ's peace.)

. . .

Perfect Joy

Francis' parable of perfect joy always used to worry me, because I felt
that it was illogical, and that any attempt to manufacture false feelings of joy in a situation of suffering would backfire in repressed
anger. My wife and I were professed as tertiaries together in 1991. In
July 2003 she was diagnosed with chronic congestion of the lungs. It
had already advanced to the point where it was inoperable and we
were told it was a matter of time before she died. A year later she
became bedridden and she died just before Christmas 2004. A
tremendous amount of prayer was offered by our church, fellow tertiaries and praying people the world over. Yet from the time of the
diagnosis, she had peace. Two things inspired her. Like Francis, she
wanted to experience the sufferings of Christ. As we know, this prayer
was answered by the gift of the stigmata to Francis. She also believed
that Jesus' death on the cross was a direct result of asphyxiation

because he became unable to lift himself up and take the strain from his arms. Thus she felt that in some small way her desire was also granted. When people came to visit her, they were usually greeted by her smile, and when they left her room, they were uplifted by her tranquility. Yes, there were times of anxiety and fear. Yet the dominant experience was the peace that passes understanding. I still worry about the parable of perfect joy because I don't display much joy in suffering. But at least I have a glimpse of what it could be.

David Bertram

.   .   .

Prayer of Penance

Lord, I pray for those with heavy crosses
who suffer for the sins of their parents
and for the sins of those born before them.
Open their eyes, Lord, so they may see suffering
as the cross you have given them to bear.
May they be guided by your humility on the road to Calvary,
sharing in the pain you bear for sinners throughout time
in this world and in purgatory,
so by your grace and their ultimate repentance
they may be with you in heaven.
Open their hearts, Lord, so your love may assist them when the devil
    lies and tries to destroy trust in those they love.
Give them courage, Lord, to endure suffering and welcome it
so they do not protect themselves by closing their heart
to the love and the wisdom of God.
Give them faith, Lord, in times when you withdraw
to test their strength and trust in you.
So they know that even in hell you are with them.

Illuminate their souls, Lord, so when you speak to them
they know it is you and not the wiles of the devil.
When you draw close may they know peace
and the comfort of your presence.
Still loving you even when you withdraw again
and leave them to face the devil alone.
If the devil destroys trust in their brothers and sisters
may they still see you in creation.
Knowing you are there in the beauty of a breeze
and the wonder of a bird in flight
in tiny creatures and in nature and in the mighty heavens
where you reign forever and ever.
Amen.

Eileen Wood

. . .

Take Up the Cross

Riding on horseback, on trains, on planes
Fleeing from pain and self
Blinded by light, deafened by silence
The passion of greed and longing
The Son of God or the Lamb of God
The beauty or the beast
The destroyed face of the leper with AIDS
And the kiss which changes all

Darkness is black and darkness is light
Death—horror and glory
You take up the cross and the cross takes you
Beyond laughter and pain—the cherub

Consummation of love—abyss of death
Bleeding body and soul
The stillness of La Verna's peak
The cries from the valley below
Back to the crowds! Become the leper!
Take up the cross to be saved
The "Cloud of Unknowing" your only treasure
Faith, hope and love
and a song of praise

M. Irmingard Thalmeier, F.N.S.

. . .

Splinters From the Cross

Little headaches, little heartaches,
Little griefs of every day. Little trials, and vexations How they throng
    around our way. One great cross; immense and heavy
So it seems to our weak will, Might be borne with resignation;
But these many small ones kill. Yet all life is formed of small things,
Little leaves make up the trees, many tiny drops of water
Blending, make the mighty seas; So these many little burdens.
Pressing on our hearts so hard, all uniting, form a life's work.
    Meriting a grand reward.
Let us not then, by impatience
Mar the beauty of the whole. But for the love of Jesus bear all,
In the silence of the soul asking him for grace sufficient,
To sustain us through each loss and to treasure each small offering
As a splinter from His Cross.

Lawrence Carroll

As I Gazed

As I gazed at your dusty and bloodstained feet,
I knew they were of a man I've yet to meet.
And as I gazed at the wound in your side,
I knew, Lord Jesus, that you had died.
And as I held your hand so warm,
I knew that your love would calm the storm.
And as I gazed into your face
that surpasses all color and race.
I saw the thorns so hard-pressed.
You, a King, who would have guessed.

Yvonne Ingham

. . .

Death

Grieving,
separation of loved ones.
Our hearts ache.
Loving God, grant them new Life in You,
And give us peace.
So be it!

Mary Jeanne Michels

FOR REFLECTION

Contemplate the story of the Passion from one Gospel.

SUGGESTED SCRIPTURE

Matthew 10:34–39; 16:24–26

NOTES

[1] Fortini, p. 548.

[2] *St. Francis of Assisi: Writings and Early Biographies (English Omnibus of Sources for the Life of St. Francis)*, Marion A. Habig, ed. (Quincy, Ill.: Franciscan Press, 1991), pp. 1429–1436. Hereafter this book will be referred to as the *Omnibus of Sources*.

[3] *Omnibus of Sources*, p. 1431.

[4] Francis undertook three periods of prayer and fasting annually—during Lent, from All Saints (November 1) until Christmas and after the Feast of the Assumption (August 15) in preparation for the Feast of Saint Michael (September 29).

[5] Those familiar with Francis' *Rule for Hermitages* will see this as an example of putting the principles into practice. Francis encouraged the brothers to spend periods of contemplation with others. They would take turns to be "mother" or "Martha," dealing with visitors and the provision of essentials while the rest of the group could have times of undisturbed silence.

[6] *Omnibus of Sources*, pp. 1433–1434.

[7] *FA:ED I*, "The Life of Saint Francis," p. 103.

FRANCIS IS OFTEN ASSOCIATED WITH ANIMALS, PARTICULARLY BIRDS. THERE are several recorded episodes describing the attraction that Francis seemed to hold for irrational creatures. We read about birds obeying his command for silence while the brothers praised God. We hear of his special love for lambs because Christ was the Lamb of God. Jesus referred to himself as a worm and not a man, so Francis took care to remove worms from pathways to protect them from being crushed. The story about taming the wolf of Gubbio is well-known.

The Canticle of the Creatures is probably the most widely known of Francis' prayers. Francis' love of creation was rooted in his spirit of prayer and his desire for unity with God. All creation praises God, who alone has the right to be praised.

Francis appreciated distinctiveness within creation and respected creatures for living as they were created to be, thus giving glory to the Father. God wills that humanity exercises just stewardship. Francis did not seek to dominate or exploit creation. Every created thing shares one Father, so all are brothers and sisters. All created things reflect the goodness and generosity of God, so contemplation of creation draws the prayer closer to God. Francis developed a deep sense of the goodness of God, high and supreme, beyond everything created.

As Francis became more intimate with God, he understood the true nature of relationships and developed a sense of justice. As part of creation, human beings have more in common with other creatures than with God. We are made in the likeness of God, but we are also the only creatures who have sinned. Sin blinded human nature, so humanity lost the instinctive ability to live in right relationship, not only with God but also with the rest of creation. Christ, through the Incarnation, reconciled and restored everything.

To be justified means to be centered and in line. For every creature this means being whatever God created it to be. Truth places God, not self, at the center of being. Grace and the will to see with new eyes are both necessary before mankind can accept the real truth.

Francis was widely renowned for his spirit of prayer. Some chapters in *The Remembrance of the Desire of a Soul* are dedicated to his prayer. Prayer made him present to heaven in spirit; he thirsted with his whole body and soul for Christ; he could separate himself from distractions, using his mantle to make a little cell, or covering his face with his sleeve, but failing this he could make a temple out of his breast; he was totally absorbed in God; he shed tears; he had conversations with his Lord. Celano summed it up when he wrote that Francis became totally a prayer.

Francis struggled greatly over whether he should become a contemplative. He prayed about this matter, before asking his brothers to help him to discern what to do, believing that he had a greater grace of prayer than of speaking. He sent a brother to Sylvester for his advice, and to Clare and her sisters, beseeching them to pray and discuss what he should do. The same answer came back from both. It was God's will that Francis preach. In response to this clear advice, he set out on the road again immediately.

Several of the witnesses, at the process of canonization for Clare, spoke about her devotion to prayer and how she appeared transformed after periods of devotion. In her writings we read the fruits of her periods of contemplation before the crucifix. She shared Francis' insight into the poverty, humility and love of the Savior.

In taking a firm stand on poverty and relationships with the brothers, Clare faced opposition from the pope. She, with her sisters, must have prayed intensely to test the spirits and determine God's will. She persevered according to the discernment that came out of her life of prayer, even though it conflicted with the papal view.

Clare later discerned that she should compose a form of life for her community, having previously accepted and tried to live according to various forms of life. She was the first woman to write a form of life and have it approved by the pope.

Clare and Francis both lived according to the spirit of fraternity and sorority, showing personal care for the sick in their communities. Personally inspired by the example of Christ and the spirit of the gospel, they followed different ways.

Contributions

Heavenly Father

Heavenly Father, Creator and Lover of all, we thank You for the great love that You inspired in the heart of Our Holy Father Saint Francis. We humbly ask you to draw us into an appreciation of all your creation, in the spirit of Francis, who was filled with wonder and awe at the beauty of the world that you have made. In response, Francis poured out his hymn of praise in The Canticle of Brother Sun, showing how his life had become filled with the sense of your presence in all things. May we too walk with reverence on our earth and may we, daily, give you glory for all that reflects you on every side. May your Spirit teach us to see your Divinity in everything human and to grow in reverence of our world with its rich variety of people and natural resources. May our enjoyment of such great gifts lead us to prayer so that, like Our Holy Father Saint Francis, we may sing a Canticle of praise.

We ask this through Our Lord, Jesus Christ, Our Redeemer, in whose Footsteps Francis walked with joy and boundless love. Amen.

Cecilia Sweeney

. . .

REFLECTION ON THE OUR FATHER

OUR FATHER WHO ART IN HEAVEN

> You are one, unity, our center
> You are the converging lens
> In you we see ourselves
> You are our mirror, our image
> You are Almighty, great, protector, provider
> You are great in depth, breadth and height
> You are above, our creator, our potter
> Mould us once again
> Provider, fill our emptiness
> To you we belong
> To you we have foundation
> In you we are secure
> In you our plan originates and ends
> You are ours and no forces
> Can take that from us

HALLOWED BE THY NAME

> May your name be made holy
> May your name be proclaimed by all creatures
> May the melodies of life proclaim your name
> May all creation recognize and own your greatness
> That all creatures may revere you

Tunelessly may your name be remembered
May your name live in the hearts of all people
May you be blessed and revered through all generations

THY KINGDOM COME
Rule in our hearts
Reign in our wills
Take control of us
Establish your throne in our hearts
Establish your reign in us
Ruler of the universe
Sovereign king of kings

THY WILL BE DONE ON EARTH AS IT IS IN HEAVEN
Give us docile hearts
Receive all we are
Receive all we give
Let us yield for you a rich harvest
Let your commands rule our lives
Give us submissive and obedient hearts
To do your will, your only will
Oh great and almighty king

GIVE US THIS DAY OUR DAILY BREAD
Jehovah Jire, the provider, provide our needs of today
Look with mercy on our daily needs
Look with favor on our necessities
May your mercy provide for your children
Kind Father, merciful savior

AND FORGIVE US OUR TRESSPASSES
Let your providing kindness provide mercy for our sins, too

Look with tolerance and forgive us
Our weaknesses that stain your name
Merciful Father, Lord of the universe
How great you are
How great is your love?

AS WE FORGIVE THOSE WHO TRESSPASS AGAINST US
You forgive us to the measure we forgive others
Loving Lord, teach us to love
Teach us to cherish others
Teach us to lift high our neighbors
That we should have humility
To think others better than us
So as to love with respect
Give us insight to see ourselves in the weakness of others
To see ourselves as you see us

AND LEAD US NOT INTO TEMPTATION
May you never ignore us in times of trial
May your mercy lift us up in difficulties
May your love remember us in times of darkness

BUT DELIVER US FROM EVIL
We cry to you for help, Lord, come to our aid
You are our Lord, our protector, our shield
You are our standard, our fortress, our rock of refuge
Come to our rescue that we may see your saving help
Be fast, our hope, and do not delay
Our citadel, our valiant in war
In the shadow of your wings we do run for refuge
In trial Lord be our protector, our defender
Our citadel, our foundation, our rock, our shield

Our pillar, our deliverer, our refuge
That your shelter shall accompany us wherever we go
Mighty in strength, powerful and gloriously enthroned king
For ever and ever. Amen.

Mary Flora Awino, F.S.J.

. . .

A Prayer of Thanksgiving

Praise to God for the morning dew, a perfect drop glistens each grass blade.

Praise to God for the tiny, soaring lark, who greets the morning with pure joy.

Praise to God for the gossamer butterfly, whose delicate wings jewel the flower.

Praise God for the trickling stream,

Clear and sparkling, between mossy banks.

Praise God for the feathery herb, Lad's love, to give a memory scent.

Praise to God for the sea-washed stone, Smoothed, shiny, tri-colored pebble.

Praise to God for the white jasmine, Sweet scent, to end the summer day.

Angela Alexander

FRUSTRATION

My God, how can I say in mere and mortal words just how vital is
    your love and care for me?

In times when prayer does not exist, or time is short and pressures
    build,

You press upon my consciousness a leaf, a drop of rain, a lovely piece
    of wood—some small, private notice of your presence and
    concern.

In times of joy and moments of excitement your constant being
    magnifies the peak.

Your gifts of seas and mountains in my life mean more than my best
    efforts can express;

And surpassing even these you give me friends, friends to love and
    care about—

And more than that, friends to show me you.

In times of pain, anxiety, and sorrow, when it's easiest to speak—out
    of my need—you never fail to hear.

This need I feel and cannot achieve. My limitations frustrate me. I
    search for ways to tell you of my love and have no words, and then
    I see it doesn't matter what I say. You know.

Sister Mary McMillan

. . .

PEACE

There's a light that dawns at daybreak
When the sun peeks over the hills;
There's a song that fills the air the moment
A meadow lark trills;

There's pleasure that comes at sunset
When clouds are streaked with gold;
And there's delight in summer
When roses first unfold.
There's rest that comes in moonglow
When silver stars are bright;
And rapture when a symphony
Lifts the soul in flight;
There's joy that comes in sowing
A tiny fertile seed;
And there's peace in giving solace
To someone in great need.

Evelyn Blanchard

. . .

MORNING PRAYER

Dear God, let me begin this day as an empty vessel. Fill me with your Grace and your Holy Spirit, and leave no room for anything else.

Let me be constant and unseen in my observance of penitence and temperance, and lead me by the hand when I falter. Help me to touch as many lives as possible, but not with my hand. Let me feel my neighbor's pain before my own; and let me love everyone I encounter, whether I like them or not.

When I am slow to relinquish the last vestige of self, take it from me and cast it into the abyss, and when the slings and arrows of my oppressors are no longer enough, help me to mortify my flesh in remembrance of your sacrifice.

I ask this through my crucified and risen Lord, always at the center of my life. Amen.

Jane Mortimer

Night Blessing

Long past midnight, friends have left.
The house is an island whose ferry has gone.
Sleep collects behind curtains, eyelids.
Lovers a hand's breadth apart dream
in separate lands. Wood tightens, creaks.
I snap the locks on the patio door,
the bolt at the back. A woodlouse treks
an expanse of kitchen floor, disappears.
I pause at a halo of wine on the table.
A tiny shock as a moth hits the lamp,
then silence, not merely the absence of sound,
closes round to the pulse of the clock.
I douse lights 'til portrait colors are still,
infilled with night, let slip each thought;
breathe His name in and out. May it bring peace.

Carol Whitfield

. . .

Night Psalm

Inside out you have gathered up the grains of me.
The arid lifeless sands of longings,
the smooth crystal remnants of my sufferings,
Worn faceless, transparent as tears.
You have showered upon your face
the shapeless silken droplets of my soul.
Finding me sweet like fruit plucked from the vine.
You have drunk of me.

Tasting, you have imbibed in my love
And then, taking the dregs of me, you have spilled them out,
Washing my feet to show me just how sweet you find me.
Raise me to your lips again O Lord,
Ebullient with kisses meant for only me.
Seize me now! Your passion drenching all of me that is not whole
In rivulets seep down into the ashen desert of my bones
and quench me with your mercy.
That born again, my face will run with tears of living water,
my lips thus moistened, praise your Holy Name.
for you have cracked the tomb around my heart, O God,
And raising it like sweet bread broken,
Have found it to be true.

Mary Zablocki

. . .

FRANCIS: A SONG FOR THE ROAD

Lord, you are all my joy.
You are all my love,
  all my passion,
  all my strength.
You are all my pleasure,
  all my delight.
You are all my fire,
  all my life.
All my sweetness,
  all my madness,
  all my longing,
  my bitter emptiness,

my sweet satisfaction,
   my ecstasy, and my peace.
You are all, and all, and all
   to me.

Susan Pitchford

. . .

You Were There

When I felt hurt and low, you were there filling me with love and understanding. When I thought life was not worth living, you were there with your sunshine challenging me to make something of myself. When I hated many and wanted to destroy them you were there reminding me that Satan could not win a battle that was fought with you inside of me. When I was sad, you were there giving me all the love required to make me feel better. When I needed forgiveness, you were there giving me support and telling me that you loved me and would forgive me. When I discovered you, you were there with your presence waiting to let me know that when I fell you would help me. When I refused to make peace, you were there making me understand peace was the best solution. When love was not enough, you were there filling my heart with more love than I had ever experienced in my life which gave me the power to endure even the most difficult paths. When many unknown paths were put in my life, you were there helping me choose the road to a joyful life. When friendship was found miles away, you were there being the friend I never knew I had. When joy filled my heart, and I wanted to keep it all to myself, you were there teaching me the way to let everyone know the good news.

Thank you, Lord for being there in my lowest and happiest hours.

Sister Olivia Rico

LORD OF MY LIFE

Lord of my life,
May I remain as a living flame,
Burning brightly in your sanctuary
As a reflection of your strength and your glory,
So that I may bring your healing love to others.
Amen.

Ann Groves

. . .

I THOUGHT ABOUT LOVE TODAY

I thought about love today
It surely made me cringe
I realize I have not given love
The way it should have been
I have been fooling myself
And yet I think I'm not
But Our Lord humbled me
So now I know the truth
I thought about love today
And now I know what to do.

Laura Jarvi

WORD

In the beginning
words
spilling over
running down
filling empty space
Then, an inkling
lurking in silence
insistent
necessary as
breath
Slowly revealed
stroke upon stroke
meaning emerges
diffuses from
center
Top to bottom
color upon color
Life in life
Word

Lynda Maraby

. . .

CANTICLE OF BROTHER AND SISTER SPORTS

Praise be to you, my Lord, for brother and sister sports which are good, wholesome, character building and fun. Come play with us Lord and enjoy our game and help us praise your Name.

Justus Wirth, O.F.M.

Harvest Autumn

I walk streets green, up avenues,

kick leaves maples golden glows,

bright as sun, touched with orange,

bind with flowers flung as bows.

I lift up leaves rain-felled,

gold is crushed in my hand hold,

leaf as veins, lines violet,

very violet, damp and cold.

My eyes find hills azure hung,

beyond the avenues of gold,

against a sky of sack-silk clouds,

with beauty barbarous and cold.

I harvest autumn, farmer I,

wagons loads of colorfest,

to fill my winter-weary barn,

my roads of time, my fields at rest.

Charles Knoll

REFLECTION

Take time to enjoy creation around you. Give wholehearted thanks
and praise to God.

SUGGESTED SCRIPTURE

Genesis 1:1—2:3

Psalms 104, 145

Isaiah 43:1-5

STATION FOURTEEN: TRANSITUS

IN THIS STATION WE SEE DEATH AS UNION WITH GOD AND ENTRY INTO NEW life. Death was welcomed by Francis and Clare, who knew they were going straight to their Lord.

The legends tell us of the extreme suffering Francis endured throughout the last two years of his life. Yet Francis praised and thanked God for the consolation he experienced through fulfilling his will by undergoing these tribulations.

It was clear that Francis was going to die soon and he asked to be taken to the Portiuncula. During his last days he found great solace and comfort from his brothers. He found that he could more easily tolerate his sufferings if some of his companions sang the praises of God. The general minister, Elias, thought this undignified behavior might cause scandal among the local people, suggesting that it was surely time to prepare for death in a nobler manner. But Francis explained that by the grace of the Holy Spirit he was so united and joined to Christ that he wanted to rejoice with the "Most High Himself."

Celano tells us that Francis was able to say to the brothers around him: "I have done what is mine; may Christ teach you what is yours."

The legends leave us in no doubt that Francis was very well prepared and truly welcomed Sister Death, while, at the same time, he was eager to give consolation to his brothers.

The glorious nature of his passing was marked by people witnessing his soul ascend into heaven, and larks gathering to rejoice above the place, even though it was already twilight on the eve of October 4, 1226.

CLARE

Francis had sent a letter of consolation to Clare before he died. She was devastated and found it hard to carry on living.

For many years she suffered physically and mentally. When the time for her own death came, on August 11, 1253, she was just as ready for death as Francis had been. On her deathbed, she received the Form of Life she had composed, sealed by Innocent IV. She died surrounded by her own community, joined by Leo, Angelo and Juniper, early and intimate companions of Francis. These brothers gave tremendous support to the distraught sisters.

She asked to hear the Passion of Christ read, blessed everyone, and brought comfort and encouragement. She was heard freeing her soul to leave her body. She then beheld a vision of the king of glory. Sister Benvenuta had a vision of the heavenly court preparing to honor Clare. There was an overwhelming spirit of peace.

At both deaths, witnesses experienced a sense of the Resurrection. This encouraged their followers to proclaim the good news, rather than wallow in grief.

CONTRIBUTIONS

TRANSITUS

Far from the every with-wind scurrying
that is the sobbing at the center of the world
we came tonight
to walk by starlight
on this quiet shore.
Very high above us Aldebaran gleamed
while, such balm to callous-tired souls,
the far sands glimmered

cool and level and firm,

ghost-touched by the wraiths of waves just guessed.

Oh, Father, Look!

look there!

caught in the sandsheen of a mercurial water-mirror

here's the bright reflection of that distant star,

momently earthed and very close.

Thus led, our passage to life could begin, and we gathered,

moth-quiet to keep vigil round an altar candlelit,

wistful because there was no soft brown humble habit

to spread, empty, on the floor;

token of another's gentle transitus.

Quickening to an anticipated coalescing, we, too, diffused,

glad to slough our much too separated selves

and real, choosing to love,

we were spendthrift spindrift

We journey now to a different rhythm

recollecting in tranquility

the taste of Christ on our tongues in the morning:

the shared see, touch, smell, ringing true sound of him,

epiphanies gracious in the telling.

And so, Francis, to our poverty,

such riches come, neither blind nor indiscriminate,

that there are no shadows

in the imminent sea-change

of our patterning of you.

D.H. Lubbe for Father Christopher Neville, O.F.M.

OH HOLY SPIRIT

Oh Holy Spirit, come down to guide us.

Lift the mist that clouds our heart and mind.

Grant us the wings to fly above earthly values.

And begin to perceive thru Grace the Path,

the only highway in which to reach our Heavenly inheritance.

We ask this through Our Lord Jesus Christ, Your Son.

Who lives and reigns with You and The Holy Spirit, One God for ever and ever. Amen.

Alban Pinkney

.   .   .

THE BEST IS YET TO COME

When I look at my relationship with the Lord and how much I need His Living Presence in my soul, I feel a longing for the day when I will see His Holy Face. I long for the Peace and Joy that is promised to those who love my Loving Lord, and I know then that the best is yet to come.

I love life as a waiting station on the way to better shores, and I long for the moment when my mission in this life is done, I know that I am impatient; so the Lord who knows me well gives me plenty of occasions to learn to wait till He comes to call.

I call those moments of agitation and restlessness my gifts from God; for they turn my thoughts and feelings toward His Presence in my soul. I give thanks also to the Holy Spirit who guides my every thought and the wishes and longings of my heart and soul.

All I ask from my Blessed Holy Trinity is to give me strength when the days are long or when my nights are full with anxious and apprehensive thoughts that come to me not welcomed and uncalled. I ask of You, Blessed Trinity, guardian of my soul, to deliver me from this turmoil when it comes to make its calls. Shelter me till the day of the Lord.

Letitia Ewbank

. . .

Transitus of Saint Clare—A Reflection

We gather together this evening as daughters and friends of our holy mother, Saint Clare, to behold her once again as she was in her earthly life in the last moment of passing to eternal life.

In doing so we slip back into history to that little dormitory at San Damiano where the sisters, weeping silently, are circled around their beloved sister as she lay dying.

For them it is a time of extreme grief. How will they ever endure without her support and encouragement as they face the daily struggles of a hard life? *Who* will point them repeatedly to the crucified ONE, reminding them that the depth of His Love is found in each other? *To whom* can they look for guidance and clarity when the initial inspiration of holy poverty and true humility becomes clouded with time? Fear, uncertainty and sorrow grip their hearts as they spend these last moments with their dying mother.

For Clare, the long awaited moment has arrived. At last, she will experience the unrelinquishing embrace of her Beloved. She will gaze upon the unveiled beauty of his face and audibly hear the tender words of love, which until now, have been only echoes of her heart! The moment of true reality is imminent! Clare is about to be totally united with her Spouse. All the years of longing, suffering, surrendering have led her to this exquisite moment of joy. Clare and her loving Lord will now be one forever. And as Clare departs, what does Clare bequeath her sisters (those around her, those down through the centuries)?

—a spirit of faith, that will enable them to find God in every human experience.

—a strong sense of sisterhood that will be for them the presence of Jesus in their midst.

—a love of poverty that will forever unite them to the poor Christ whose love knows no limits.

—a strong desire for prayer that will nurture and sustain them through even the darkest hours.

—a passionate love of Jesus that will call them to identification with the crucified one, and in doing so, will find the truth of their own identity as mirrors of Jesus Christ, poured out for others.

Let us now place ourselves at San Damiano to be present with Clare and her sisters on this last eve of her life.

Sister Doreen Trautman, O.S.C.

. . .

FRANCIS' FINAL REVERIE: A REFLECTION

As the doves replaced the larks by cooing the opening of a new day,
Francis was heard to finish his prayer of the night and All could hear
   him say,
MY GOD AND MY ALL!
He rose in his mind and viewed the valley, the horizon, the cloud-
   less sky, under which he loved to dwell. There were Olive trees and
   poppies, grass, hills and dales as Far as one could tell!
MY GOD AND MY ALL!
Though the years had left him somewhat shaken while God,

Himself, Francis, had overtaken, his mind was clear, his heart was
pure, his love remained steadfast, single-minded and sure.

MY GOD AND MY ALL!

His longing for the life beyond consumed him now As never before.

Each new day was another chance to increase his Heavenly score.

MY GOD AND MY ALL!

Often his mind wandered to the wonders of his life. How God had
chosen him...with poverty as his wife. God seemed to enjoy his
impish, childish, prank-filled days All the while carving him into
Godlike ways.

MY GOD AND MY ALL!

He also thought of the wonder of Lady Clare.

Perhaps if he went to the monastery she would greet him there.

They could review the mystery of God's simplicity

To call them to be present, one day, with his Majesty.

MY GOD AND MY ALL!

He recalled the winter when he had decided

To break away from these nuns whom he guided

Whose spiritual lives were beyond compare

While their devotion and love filled him with despair.

What had he to give them that they already did not possess

They who knew so well the great secret of holiness.

MY GOD AND MY ALL!

And, Clare, the greatest witness of all God's works

Pleaded with him on that winter day

And, yes, Francis said he would return that way

When the roses were blooming on the bushes once again

Lo, how God answered Clare's prayer with roses right then!

MY GOD AND MY ALL!

His reverie was interrupted by the sound of a familiar voice

He recognized the woman outside who had made a special choice
To follow Francis in her own style...Lady Jacoba...
Now called Brother, came to visit with Francis for awhile.
Her handiwork she brought as a garment for a king,
The rough and shapeless gown and cowl with a three knotted string.
The cookies Francis only tasted, for heavenly food did he now require,
All present understood and were inflamed by his desire.
MY GOD AND MY ALL!
After praying many prayers together, Francis called his first son.
Upon him gave a blessing such as the Old Testament leaders would have done.
Then he asked for the "Canticle" by Brother Angelo to be sung.
Angelo coughed and choked a bit in between, but kept the melody as one.
Francis rejoiced in hearing it sung so well and he blessed his brother
In his small cell.
Just as the music came to an end, a shout was heard outside.
Elias quickly came into the dwelling where Francis did abide.
"Now Brother, won't the townspeople be shocked upon the eve of your departure to hear music? It must be stopped!"
To complain about singing the Canticle of great love For the one who had composed it was a bit absurd! But the one for who it had been sung, lay dying.
And looking up at Elias, he just began sighing!
MY GOD AND MY ALL!
And, so, Francis passed through to the other side from that very site
While all the birds sang, whether they usually sang in darkness or light!
The bells from Saint Stephen's joined in this great song.

The people from the village came to see what was wrong.
They formed an army no monarch had ever had
And formed a procession more regally clad
Than any Assisi had ever seen...
Francis had gone to meet his Poverty Queen.
MY GOD AND MY ALL!

Frances Thom

. . .

BE YOUR "GREATEST EVER"

THOSE WHO ARE INTERESTED IN A CERTAIN ART OR SKILL OR SPORT WILL TALK at length about who is the greatest in that field. Each line of human endeavor has its heroes, its own little inner circle of top achievers. In sports we have the Hall of Fame.

Excitement breathes over the possible discovery of the "greatest ever," the best singer, the perfect athlete, the peerless artist.

Some men and women, some children, are top achievers in the highest category of human endeavor: love of God and man. They are top people in bringing to a happy fulfillment the word of Christ: Be perfect as your heavenly Father is perfect. The Church has two Halls of Fame for them. One is called Beatification, the other Canonization. Those chosen for these Halls are called Blessed and Saint.

One day or a future day may produce even greater saints. There is one among them however, who will never be surpassed. She was the best possible woman God Himself could create within the limits of his plans for mankind. Her name is Mary. She humbly avoided the superlative, yet under divine inspiration predicted: All generations shall call me blessed.

Some ages have "discovered" her more than others, and the joy and excitement of the "greatest ever" have spilled over onto fragile canvas and enduring stone, into exquisite word-patterns of a multitude of languages.

When you really discover Mary, you also discover in a new way the One for whom God created her and all of us. He stands at the head of all creation, visible and invisible. First in the creative blueprints of God was the humanity of Jesus. All other persons and things were made for Him because in him perfect creaturehood was joined to divinity. As we proclaim at the climax of the Eucharistic Prayer: Through Him, with Him, in Him all glory and honor is yours, Almighty Father.

Our hope for loving God and man in the best way lies in following Him. Our hope for ourselves reaching the top as persons lies in being united to Jesus, the Perfect Man. Mary, His mother, and Joseph, the virgin-father and all the great servants of God, the saints, help us come to Him. They are models and guides along the way. Jesus is the Way, the Truth, the Life.

Nowhere does He show us the way more than in His Passion. Even Jesus, the God-man, reached the fullness of perfect manhood only in the complete giving of Himself to God the Father by suffering and dying.

The joy of reaching our own "best ever" must come from taking up our cross daily and following Him. This is the real challenge and excitement of living. The Passion of Jesus is not isolated history. It is a daily call from His cross, begging us to love as He did.

But to love as He did implies winning freedom from the hindering drag of unruly self-love. In turn this means doing the duties of our state of life. It means prayer and penance, endless adaptation to and forgiveness of others. If you want to be perfect within the limits of the distinctive, individual human nature God gave you, if you want to be tops in loving God and man, learn from the crucifix.

Father Christopher, O.F.M. CAP.

. . .

LITANY OF SAINT FRANCIS

Response: Saint Francis, Pray for us
joyful poverello
happy troubadour
in harmony with the Spirit
powerful in perseverance
respecting stigmata of Jesus
lover of creation
lover of God
lover of Mary
lover of scripture
lover of church
respecter of church authority
vowed in poverty
vowed in chastity
vowed in obedience
diligent/humble in serving poor
example of life for brothers
example of life for Clare/sisters
fraternally loved by his brothers
man of vision
man of action
man of contemplation
mirror of poverty

possessed by God's grace
intimate lover of God
exemplar of kindness/generosity
sojourner on Mt. Alverna
inspiration for Franciscan action
in soul's search for God
in his mystic union with God
gifted with preaching
gifted with peace making
gifted with stigmata
gifted with wisdom in suffering
believed all saved by Word of God
believed we see Jesus here in Eucharist
believed in devotion to Blessed Sacrament
believed in passion uniting us to Jesus
believed unity with Jesus so as to reproduce His life in us
believed Eucharist/scripture led to Franciscan spirit
believed in community of servants working way to God
believed devotion to Mary led to closeness to God
believed God is our Father, Lord and Master of our life
believed in the great mercy of God
believed we should have a thankful spirit at all times
exemplar of simplicity
exemplar of unity
observer of the Gospel
dependent on union with God
attracted to poverty
intoxicated with God
awakening others to the peace of God
preaching peace to all

knowing peace is the dwelling place of God

through wings of seraph possessed with progress in peace

final peace, love of Crucified

groaning in prayer through Christ Crucified

Ramona Kruse

· · ·

O Lord

O Lord, guide us who try to follow in the footsteps of our holy father Francis.

Help us to look after the poor and needy, as he did, and to use our time in your service.

Francis loved your holy mother Mary, we consecrate ourselves to her so that she may use us as she desires to do your holy will.

Lord soothe the suffering, bless the dying, release the holy souls in purgatory.

Fill us with your spirit Lord, so that we may make our way in your grace.

Thank you for all the graces and blessings you have bestowed on us.

Eileen Kates

· · ·

A Prayer to Saint Francis

Gentle Saint Francis

Teach us to love as you love

When we meet our lepers

May we see in them the face of Christ

When we meet our wolves
May we forgive them
And feed their hunger
Both bodily and spiritual
Teach us to love the crèche
For who and what it represents
The tender babe who was born to be our Savior
Lovingly cared for by Mary and Joseph
Pure and obedient
Encourage us to rebuild God's church
With bricks and mortar
With prayer and exhortation
And most of all
With love
Amen

Carol Maffettone

. . .

SAINT FRANCIS OF ASSISI

Francis was a merchant's son
His wealthy life secure
Courtly ball and battles won
His social status sure.
But he felt the stirrings in his life
And saw visions in the night
Lady Poverty would be his wife
And the Gospel be his light.
Young Francis heard, the cross did speak
Calling him to toil
To help rebuild the Church so weak

Its neglect and sin did spoil.
Stone on stone, his body sore
But the heaviest burden lifted—
His sinful past, the Lord he bore
And a saint the world He gifted
There was a girl who came to give
Her sisters to be poor
Clare her name she would live
A life of prayer, her Lord adore.
Soon other men desired to live
In penitence so bare
All their wealth was theirs to give
And lepers were their care.
The birds in praise rejoiced
And the beasts on land bowed low
To hear their names being voiced
By these poor friars below.
Their numbers grew at such a rate
That Francis made a Rule
And went before the Church and State
And danced just like God's fool.
So he sent them out, two by two
To the corners of the land
Still the Order grew and grew
Soon their property was grand.
To La Verna, Francis did despair
Lady Poverty had been forsaken
The Seraph came to meet him there
And with the marks of Christ was laden.
Francis took the cross upon himself

In hands and feet and side
The pain of Christ became his wealth
And for the love of man he cried.
Soon the world it loved him dear
As an example of our way
Always keeping Christ so near
Until He meets us on that day.

Andrew Wilkes

.   .   .

Brother Francis

Brother Francis, Brother Francis
If you were here today
How would you be serving God
What would you do and say?
And Francis would reply:
I would be caring for the dying
And those with AIDS and HIV,
I would be seeking out the homeless
Feeding the starving refugee
Brother Francis, Brother Francis
If you were alive today
How would you be loving God
What would you do and say?
I would visit all the prisons
Keep watch throughout the night,
Share with them in Christ's agony
Until the morning light
Brother Francis, Brother Francis

If you were alive today
How would you be serving God
What would you do and say?
I would speak out against abortion
And speak up for those who cannot speak
I would not go to work
And would turn the other cheek
Brother Francis, Brother Francis
If you were alive today
How would you be loving God
What would you do and say?
I would be a popstar in a popstar band
Writing protest songs
Doing gigs throughout the land
I would go on protest marches
Speak up for the right to life
From conception to the grave
I would pay the ultimate price.
Brother Francis, Brother Francis
If you were alive today
How would you live your life for God
What would you do and say?
In the world of today
Where there is so much greed
I would have no silver or gold
For God would provide my needs.

Elizabeth Cornell

FOR REFLECTION

Take time to remember a loved one who has passed on. Reflect on the Transitus of either Francis or Clare.

SUGGESTED SCRIPTURE

Revelation 21